The Evolution of Ideals of Womenhood in Indian Society

THE EVOLUTION OF IDEALS OF WOMENHOOD IN INDIAN SOCIETY

by

Chandra Bali Tripathi

Translation:

Chandra Mauli Mani

Publications

KALPAZ PUBLICATIONS

DELHI-110 052

The Evolution of Ideals of Womanhood in Indian Society

ISBN : 81-7835-425-X

Published in 2005 in India by
Kalpaz Publications,
C-30, Satyawati Nagar,
Delhi-110 052
E-mail : kalpaz@hotmail.com

Lasertype Setting by: Tact Computer Graphics, Delhi
Printed at: Salasar Imaging Systems, Delhi

b. 21st Nov. 1893 Pt. Chandra Bali Tripathi (Author) d. 5th Jan. 1985

In Loving Memory of My Revered Parents –
Late Pt. Chandra Bali Tripathi
and
Late Smt. Durgavati Tripathi

Contents

List of Illustrations

Preface

We have inherited hundreds of treatises written from time to time for achieving specific purposes. It is, therefore, difficult to harmonise the main thought process accumulated over thousands of years with the versions adopted within specific contexts. The result is that many enthusiasts have been holding some specific quote of a specific treatise as the sole exponent of Indian Thought, giving rise to undesirable *samskaras* amongst the public at large. Many a time even the discerning have been finding it difficult to keep clear of these.

I am delighted to see that Tripathiji has tried to get at the crux of the Indian literature, and adopting the right perspective, has successfully unfolded the kaleidoscope of woman's personality, her rights and responsibilities. This is certainly in keeping with his experience and erudition. Using the base of the subject under reference, he has, in fact, highlighted the ever developing aspect of Indian culture.

There is no gainsaying the fact that no civilization or culture would have been possible in the world without the woman. The woman, in varying roles, has provided encouragement, power and growth to the man and has succeeded in guiding him towards culture. That is why the woman is considered to be the guardian of cultural advancement of human societies. Manu, the great social scientist, had this in mind when he decreed that gods dwelt where women were worshipped. The long history of India has seen many ups and downs in the status of women and so has our culture. The author has taken cognizance of these ups and downs. He has dwelt upon the traditions, customs and laws pertaining to women in different ages. He has been equally analytical of the modern trends and has not stuck to the traditional views. In fact, he is all praise for the progressive attitude of women in modern India. He writes— "The achievement of the modern woman does not end up here— The fact that men in modern India never placed any obstacles in the path of advancement of women; rather encouraged them, is a fitting reply to the assertion of the ignorant lot who think that women have the lowest place in Indian culture." However, Tripathiji is cautious and does not approve of blind aping of the West by our womenfolk, hankering after property of the father and mad rush for jobs. He considers *sagotra* and *samapravara* marriages against Indian culture and is also not happy with the Divorce laws. In short, he takes a very balanced view of the entire subject.

Tripathiji has taken the past, present and the future in his stride. He views the past critically, has a stringent standard for the present and is carefully optimistic about the future.

I heartily welcome the book. I am confident that the book will find a hearty response amongst the well wishers of the society and the literature.

Chandigarh **(Padma Vibhushana)**

15-3-66 **Hazari Prasad Dwivedi**

A Word from the Translator

It is a matter of unique privilege for me to undertake Translation of the renowned Hindi book of my revered father, Late Pandit Chandra Bali Tripathi,—"*Bharatiya Samaj mein Nari Adarshon ka Vikas*". He was an erudite scholar of Sanskrit, History and Indian Philosophy and has enriched the Hindi literature with his monumental work—'*Upanishad Rahasya*', and many others like, '*Dharmaraja Yudhishthira*', and the present one. Many scholars, who knew about the Hindi book, suggested to me that if it could be brought out in English, it would help in expanding awareness of our glorious past and its traditions in the country and outside too. It is with this objective that I decided to embark upon this significant task, which was also a matter of great honour to me.

The book covers the vast gamut of our Ancient Indian History in so far as it has a bearing on the position of women in the society. It quotes extensively from ancient as well as modern sources in support of his views, applies incisive logic and does not take anything for granted. It is really amazing how every aspect has been dealt with so exhaustively. The author has a very open mind. Though steeped in our ancient culture and traditions, he does not accept anything blindly, not even *shastric* versions. At the same time he does not denigrate modern ideas and beliefs, provided these are healthy for the society. Here we have a book which places the whole gamut of position of women in the society in the right perspective, which is neither orthodox nor pseudo-modern.

The book is immensely readable and informative. It will be of interest to scholars as well as the general reader. For the convenience of general readers I have not used diacritical marks, which is the usual practice for books of this genre. The spellings of Sanskrit words are, however, entirely in keeping with the correct diction.

Efforts have been to ensure that the translation does not miss out on any of the facts or ideas. At the same time fluency and readability aspects have also not been ignored. Translation has some inherent drawbacks. I would, therefore, crave the indulgence of knowledgeable readers to treat the deficiencies as my fault and not judge the great work of the author adversely on that account.

I shall be failing in my duty if I do not express my gratitude to my wife, Sharda Mani, who has been the inspiration behind the effort. She was a source of strength all along in encouraging me to get on with the job with enthusiasm. Our three children, who are all well settled, and their spouses have been instrumental in ensuring atmosphere congenial to this type of endeavour. Our son, Sudhindra Mani Tripathi, and daughter, Sunanda Gaur, both settled in U.S.A. have been specially helpful in providing the necessary assistance when the writing and editing etc. were being done by me during our stay in U.S.A. with them. My elder brother, CC. Mani, and younger brothers, C.B.Tripathi and C.D.Tripathi have been extending their brotherly affection and support. Thanks are also due to Edward Pias of Davis, U.S.A. for helping me occasionally with the computer during the editing work.

The publishers deserve my sincere thanks for having brought out the book so nicely.

This humble effort of mine has been possible only with the unsolicited blessings of my parents, Late Pt. C.B.Tripathi, the author of the original, and Late Smt. Durgavati Tripathi. I shall consider it a great honour if I am able to spread the author's message through this book of his.

North Brunswick, NJ, U.S.A.

Deepavali, 2003 **Chandra Mauli Mani**

Abbreviations

Ap. Dh. Sutra	Apastamba Dharmasutra
Asht.	Ashtadhyayi of Panini
Ashva. Gr.	Ashualayana Grihyasutra
Ath. Veda/ Atharva	Atharvaveda
Baudh. Dh. Shastra	Baudhayana Dharmashastra
Bhag.	Shrimadbhagavata
Brih. Up./ Br. Up.	Brihadaranyopanishad
Chhand. Up.	Chhandogyopanishad
Devi. Bh.	Devi Bhagavata
Garbh. Up.	Garbhopanishad
Harita Dh.	Harita Dharmashastra
Isha. Up.	Ishavasyopanishad
Katha. Up.	Kathopanishad
Kumara. Sam.	Kumarasambhava of Kalidasa
M.B./ Mah. Bh./ M. Bh.	Mahabharata
Maitr. Sam.	Maitrayani Samhita
Mal.	Malavikagnimitra of Kalidasa
Manu.	Manusmriti
Mun. Up.	Mundakopanishad
Raghu.	Raghuvamsha of Kalidasa
Rig/Rg.	Rigveda
Shak.	Shȧkuntalam of Kalidasa
Shat. Br./ Sh. Br.	Shatapatha Brahmana

Tat. Up.	Tattariyopanishad
Tatt. Brah.	Tattariya Brahmana
Uttara Ram.	Uttara Ramacharita of Bhavabhuti
Va. Ram.	Valmikiya Ramayana
Vaj. Brah.	Vajasaneya Brahmana
Vishnu Pur.	Vishnu Purana
Yajna. Sm.	Yajnyavalkya Smriti
Yaju.	Yajurveda

A Preview

The Author of the Hindi Book has conjured up a kaleidoscopic vision of the entire gamut of status of women, with its ups and downs through the ages, in the Indian society in a very lucid and convincing manner. He has dealt in detail with the position of Indian women in her journey through life; pinpointing areas of inter action with the male counterpart and with the society, in general. In the process he has highlighted her unique contribution to the social infrastructure and the position of pre-eminence enjoyed by her towards the advancement of society, in general, and the family, in particular. Side by side, he has dwelt at length on the pitfalls and the dark areas that had blurred her image of excellence on account of forces of base human instincts.

The very first Chapter of the Book has meticulously defined the essentials of Indian culture and the way it has stood as a beacon-light for the civilized humanity right from the hoary past. The author quotes extensively from ancient sources to establish how the Indian culture has been unique in defining the *purusharthas—dharma, artha, kama* and *moksha*—and how our social scientists have meticulously tried to ingrain the high ideals in the society at large, with an eye on the predominant role of the women. The role of the system of *ashramas* towards realization of the higher objectives has also been clearly defined. In a nut-shell, taking a holistic view of the human existence, the role of *dharma* in refining the culture in the society has been convincingly highlighted.

The next Chapter attempts to weigh the comparative Role of Man and Woman in the Social Development Cycle. While doing so, the author emphasizes the Vedic concept of identity of the man and the woman. He goes on to establish through the authority of our sacred literature like, the *Upanishads, Dharmasutras* etc. how the ancient Indian thought has evolved around this central dictum. He holds that outwardly differences, physical and mental, are at best superficial.

Chapter III deals with the Basis of Marriage and how important it was in ancient times to ensure equal participation of the husband and wife in religious rites, which were the backbone of a dynamic society. It highlights the onus of ensuring continuity of the race as a religious and social obligation as distinct from the individualistic approach.

Chapter IV is about the Position of Women in Society. In our ancient literature women have been looked upon as forms of goddesses on account of their proficiency in arts and science. She has been described as the embodiment of knowledge and prowess, giver of *dana* (charities), unending peace and prosperity. The author quotes extensively for *Upanishads, Dharmashastras, Manusmriti, Mahabharat, Panchantantra, Uttara Ramacharita, Valmikiya Ramayana* etc. to establish that women enjoyed a highly respectable status in those days, barring a few aberrations here and there, specially in the *Mahabharata* period. Side by side, the author does not hesitate in quoting the *Vedas* and *Manusmriti,* where these have been highly critical of women of lax moral character. A critical appraisal of the thinking in society is a hallmark of the author.

In this Chapter the author deals at length with the knotty question of preference to the son over the daughter and even undesirability of the latter in Hindu society. He blasts the prevalent misconception on the subject with detailed quotations the ancient literature. As an example, the *mantra* in the *Rigveda* that the 'same pleasure which the father gets from a son is enjoyed by the mother from the daughter, rather much more', should suffice to clear the doubts. Similarly in the Epic age, there is the example of Gandhari who desires to have a daughter, even after having a hundred sons. So is the example of the Brahmana of Ekachakra who had refused to send his daughter to the demon Baka as his food in preference to his sons inspite of pleadings of the daughter. The example of love of the ascetic Kanva for his adopted daughter, Shakuntala, is too well-known.

Chapter V deals with Motherhood, Child Rearing and *Samskaras*. The author has described the role of the mother in the earliest education of the child when it imbibes *samskaras*. He rightly contrasts it with the modern tendency to leave the child at the mercy of a maid at this stage. The continuity of the role of the mother in child rearing is well bought out in this chapter, as also her contribution in planting desirable *samskaras* in the child.

The author goes on to describe with solid examples, how the *samskaras* begin getting formed right from the embryonic stage and how these get rooted continuously through the agency of the mother. Even specific knowledge gets transmitted to the embryo as in the case of Abhimanyu. Here the author has gone in detail into the ancient science of phases of development of the child during the embryonic stage itself and how external factors are seen to have had tremendous impact on its later life. The role of the mother as a life-long guide in imparting desirable qualities, like truthfulness and courage etc, has been stressed through the famous examples of Jabala (mother of Satyakama); Suniti (mother of Dhruva): Kunti, Vidula, Jeejabai (Mother of Shivaji) and even Gandhiji's mother in modern times.

Chapter VI is about the Basis of Social Evolution, comprising of *varna, ashrama* and Education. The author here propounds how education and *samskaras* in India have developed on the lines of the *varnashrama dharma*, which is essentially based on individual capabilities and stages of life. He next deals with the system of education in ancient times. The *gurukulas* were residential schools run by *rishis* at their *ashramas* and the stress was on holistic education. In post Epic age there were large universities for higher education; the most renowned ones being at Takshashila and Ujjain and later, at Nalanda, Vallabhi and Vikramashila. Details of great centres of learning at Kashi and Mithila during the Upanishadic times and *Vidyapithas* at Ayodhya, Pataliputra, Kanchi, Dhara, Tanjore etc. in later times have been given. Women desirous of higher learning were not barred from these. The author throws light on how the study of *Vedas* with complete adherence to celibacy was the cardinal feature.

The author has dealt with the controversial subject of Women and Vedic studies in the Vedic and post-vedic periods in a scholarly manner. He has brought out how in the hey day of Vedic civilization women were not only free to study the *Vedas*, but they even participated in political institutions, like *sabhas* and *samitis* and religious conferences, like *vidathas* at the time of *yajnas*. Syllabus and field of education have also been discussed. Many examples of women excelling in different fields of education like, philosophy, poetry, art etc. appear in the narrative.

Chapter VII covers Types of Marriage, its Finality and Age and Characteristics of the Bride and the Groom. The Vedic religion lays down attainment of *svarga* (heaven) through *yajnas* and that the same had to be performed along with the wife. The institution of marriage had, therefore, been central to vedic throught and practice. The *Dharmashastras* laid down lofty ideals of marriage, but without ignoring the gap in intellectual and moral standards in society. Accordingly, marriages were classified as desirable, average and outright discardable.The author describes the eight types of marriages detailed in the *Smritis* and the *Mahabharata*. Various aspects, like love marriage as understood today vis-à-vis its form and content in early times and pre-eminence of the concept of finality of marriage are duly commented upon. The institution of *swayamvara* as obtaining in various epochs has attracted the author's narrative prominently.

The next Chapter deals with Ideals of Marriage - monogamy and *pativratya* (faithfulness to the husband). On the one hand, examples of *ekapatnivratas* (devoted to one wife), like Nala and Rama have been cited. On the other, cases of *pativratas*, like Parvati, Savitri, Damayanti, Sukanya, Sita, Gandhari, Draupadi and Amba have been discussed at length, highlighting their trials and tribulations in the path of *pativratya*. *Pativratas* were held in the highest regard.

Chapter IX discusses Polyandry, Polygamy, *Anuloma* and *Pratiloma Vivahas* (marriages). While on the uncommon practice of polyandry the much talked about case of Draupadi has been discussed at length. Further, the less known fact of polygamy even amongst *rishis* has been brought to light. The author also explains the implications of *savarna* and *asavarna* (*anuloma* and *pratiloma*) *vivahas* at length.

Chapter X deals with Widow Remarriage and *Niyoga*. To start with, the author establishes in a most erudite manner how widow remarriage in the sense as we know today, was not sanctioned by the *shastras*. But he goes on to clarify how, with the laxity in moral standards, it became necessary to permit widow remarriage in modern times. This chapter throws light on the less known practice of *niyoga* resorted to in ancient times under specific conditions and with specific stipulations.

The next Chapter deals with the custom of *sati*. The author traces the history of the custom from Vedic times onwards. He thinks that the practice was not bad in the past, being voluntary, and cites cases of Madri in

Mahabharata and the *Jauhars* of the Rajput queens in mediaval times. But he agrees that the abolition of this custom by an Act of Law in the 19th century did have a salutary effect on society.

Chapter XII covers the Role of the Woman in the Family, Social and Economic Provisions, *Stree Dhana* and Succession. The high esteem in which women were held in ancient Indian society would be amply clear from the observation in the *Manusmriti*—'The family, where women feel miserable, gets destroyed soon. Where they are happy, it prospers. Gods dwell in families where women are respected, and where they are insulted, the religious rites performed by the family members go waste'. The pivotal role of the lady of the house in the well-being of the entire family is aptly stressed. The author has quoted profusely from *Valmikiya Ramayana*, *Ramacharita Manasa* of Tulasidasa, *Shakuntalam* of Kalidasa and *Manusmriti* etc. to highlight the predominant part played by women in ensuring peace and harmony and general welfare of the family. The part played by women in development of cottage industries through the ages, right up to the *Charkha* movement of Mahatma Gandhi, has been aptly dealt with.

The chapter deals with *streedhana* and rights of succession for women as per Hindu Law. Specific provisions in the *Mitakshara* and *Dayabhaga* have been explained clearly.

Chapter XIII is about the Women in Hindu Polity. It traces the part played by women in the political activities of the nation from the Vedic to the modern times. The author cites umpteen cases of ably performed Regency by the mother during minorship of the heir-apparent. Prominent among these are Satavahana Queen Nayanika (2nd cen. BC), Wakataka Queen Prabhavati Gupta (4th cen. AD), Chalukya Queen Vijaya Bhattarika (7th cen. AD) etc. Examples of Gupta Queen Kumaradevi, Rajyashri (Harsha's sister) Minaldevi, Queen Durgavati, Rani Lakshmi Bai etc. are no less prominent.

Chapter XIV deals with the subject of Woman in Indian Art. The excavations at Harappa pertaining to the Indus Valley Civilization bring out the earliest evidence of woman in Indian Art in the shape of terracotta statues of Mother Goddess. The Copper statue of a dancing girl found at Mohen-jo-daro is also unique in itself. A nude female figure carved on a Gold leaf, said to be of Mother Goddess, belonging to the 8th or 9th cen. BC is indicative of deployment of artistic states in religious practice. The Ardhanarishwara image of Mahadeva and Parvati, each in half, symbolizing the Paramatma (Almighty) and Shakti (Primordial Power) are examples of the religious and spiritual base in the early stages of Indian Art.

The depiction of woman in the form of a *yakshini* is very common. *Yakṣhini* images of the Mauryan (4th-3rd cen BC) and Shunga (2nd cen. BC.) periods and those found at the Kankali Tila are unique in artistic depiction of women. A statue found at Amaravati depicts women worshipping the lotus and the footprints symbolic of the Buddha's birth. The famous *torana* (gateway) at Sanchi (2nd-1st cen. BC) shows two elephants offering water with their trunks on Mayadevi, mother of the Buddha. The Bhita plaque of the Shunga period depicts a scene from the drama *Shakuntalam.* Certain statues belonging to the Shunga period throw light on the dresses and ornaments of women in those days. Amongst many examples the exquisite female head housed in Mathura museum does need a special mention.

Apart from being exquisite examples of Art in sculpture, these throw light on female hair styles and dresses and various dance styles. In addition, murals at Badami (6th cen AD), Ellora and Kanchipuram (8th cen. AD) etc. are fine examples of women in this art form. The most exquisite examples of *shadanga* (six constituents) *chitrana* (depiction) as defined by **Vatsyayana** in his *Kama Sutra* are to be found in Ajanta murals.

The author has, however, limited the theme to the Hindu period of our history.

Chapter XV details the spiritual achievement of Women in our society. The author has highlighted the galaxy of *rishikas* (woman recluses) in the Vedic and Upanishadic periods. He then goes onto their contribution to spirituality in the Epic period and the subsequent Buddhist period. Mention is made of prominent *bhikshunis* like, Prajapati Gautami, Amrapali, Sanghamitra Theri. The *Therigatha,* a composition of seventy *theris,* is a virtual compendium of their spiritual practices. The author gives a detailed list of *bhikshuni-shravikas* as well. The same has been done in respect of Jain nuns.

Last but not the least is the gallaxy of women saints in the Bhakti cult. This tradition went on without interruption in the south and during the mediaeval period in the North, including Maharashtra and Gujrat.

The next chapter deals with Impediments to Social Development in the form of Dowry and Purdah systems. The author has analysed in critical manner the practice of *kanya shulka* (bride price) and how it came to be looked down upon in an early age itself. Similarly, he has dealt with the practice of *yautuka* (dowry) as it existed in the beginning and how it turned to be a cancer of society in modern times, the voluntary aspect having given way to rank greed. The background behind the passing of the Anti-Dowry Act 1961, has also been covered.

The author then goes on to deal with the beginnings of the purdah system in the mediaeval period and how it resulted in exclusion of women from the social scene. He contrasts this with the highly enlightened ancient Indian society where women had excelled in all fields of social and cultural activities.

Chapter XVII covers the Practical Aspect of Freedom of Women in Society. The *Manusmriti,* which has been guiding social behaviour through the ages after the Vedic and Epic periods, lays down that every man should endeavour that the women in the household are kept under control and so on. This has been a subject of severe criticism of Indian culture. The author, in a very erudite manner, has brought to light the circumstances under which restrictions had to be placed in society. The gamut of facts and arguments is such that the subject can be appreciated only by going over the text fully.

Chapter XVIII deals with the Women in the Modern Age. The author starts with the Renaissance brought about by savants, like Raja Ram Mohan Roy, Swami Dayanada Saraswati etc. Then he goes on to the contribution made by women in modern India, like Annie Besant, Hemant Kumari Devi, Ramabai, revolutionaries like Vinodini Devi, Sarojini etc. and Col. Lakshmi of the I.N.A. The role of women in the political field has been exemplary starting with Kastur Ba Gandhi and going on to Sarojini Naidu, Vijayalakshmi Pandit, Sucheta Kripalani and Indira Gandhi Women writers likes, Subhadra Kumari Chauhan, and Ashapurna Devi, Mahadevi Verma have left their mark in the literary field.

At the same time the author does not fail to notice the tendency among modern women to ape the West in matters of dress and living style etc. He is also wary of the ill effects of liberal application of the Divorce Law.

The last Chapter is about comparative position of women in world civilizations. It covers:

Ancient Civilizations: Greece, Egypt, Rome, Persia, Semities, China, Japan, Korea and India. World Religions: Christianity, Islam, Judaism. Ancient Tribes and Races: Slavic, Celtic, Teutonic.

The narrative covers the status of women in detail in all aspects—education, legal rights, marriage customs, specific traditions—and how the situation in a particular society has been changing with the times. It provides very useful comparison amongst world societies, past and present.

In the end an exhaustive comparison has been made with the situation prevailing in the past and present Indian society so far as women are concerned. Even a cursory reading would go to indicate how primitive the status of women has been in most of the world societies when contrasted with that in India. The uniqueness of evolution of ideals of womenhood in Indian society can not be missed.

Introductory
(By the Author of the Hindi Book)

When a group of people form a society by binding themselves in a purposeful organization governed by enlightened beliefs and laws, which lay down basic duties and responsibilities, culture is born. Civilization and culture are inter dependent and inseparable. Culture develops and grows into various subtle and coarse forms of thought processes and creativity of human race. We can not restrict it to a narrow dogma or belief, because its sphere is very wide and pervasive. Economic, moral, religious, physical, political and spiritual elements are inherent in the social and cultural development. The lack of any of these elements can downgrade a culture. The soul of an advanced culture is mirrored in the development of these elements. This is absolutely true in the context of Indian culture.

According to the eternal laws of nature, a society endowed with even the highest cultural attributes does not remain great for ever. History testifies that due to human weaknesses and laxity as well as retrograde tendencies of men and women constituting a society, it loses its existence even after attaining heights of excellence. The stability and importance of the society depends on the nature of its culture. The more a society is based on exalted and eternal laws and cohesive ingredients, the more it will tend to be stable.

When we survey the Indian social scenario, we observe with astonishment that whereas many ancient civilizations of the world have disappeared, our society still draws inspiration and strength from the basic concepts and philosophies of life which had been evolved by our ancestors thousands of years ago. Verily, it is the outcome of their skilful planning. This, however, does not mean that our society has always been moving within the ambit of certain set laws. Our thinkers have been reorienting it according to the needs of the times through necessary reforms. At the same time we find that an institution or regulation that had been conducive to improvement in the society in the past became detrimental to it with changing circumstances. Nevertheless, our culture has certain elements that set apart our society from others and which are such that Bharat will not remain Bharat if these are excluded.

Culture is the most precious heritage of a country or society which binds the constituents of the nation together and makes it strong, living and eternal. A civilized person can justly be proud of it A close review of its nature, rise and fall, should be an inalienable part of the history of a nation and should act as a lighthouse of inspiration for guiding the future of the individual and the society.

A very important part of this process is the commendable contribution of women in the evolution of Indian culture from the dawn of civilization, which projects itself in the establishment of ideals for the individual and the family and in the prosperity of the society and the nation. The society has also responded by according a place of honour to the women. Human weaknesses and failings, whether in men or in women, are not true indicators or constituents of a culture. Therefore, while an analysis thereof is essential in order to alert the society, denigrating the society and its culture would be just like Miss Mayo's book, 'Mother India', which Mahatma Gandhi had condemned as a 'drain inspector's report.'

Keeping these factors in view, an effort has been made in this book to present the Evolution of Ideals of

Womanhood in the light of Indian culture from the Rigvedic times to the present day. Indian culture is fathomless, like the ocean, loftier than the Himalayas and very ancient. Till a chronological and complete history of this culture is written, it is hoped that the book will partly fill the bill. An effort has been made that all the opinions and stipulations regarding a matter taken up in this book are based on authority, and accordingly, apart from quotes from the original text, a reference has been given in the footnotes. I am confident that this book will be welcome amongst the general readers as well as students of Indian culture and Sociology.

I am extremely grateful to Padmavibhushana Dr. Hazari Prasad Dwivedi, Tagore Professor of Indian Literature and Head of Department of Hindi at the Punjab University, for according great value to the book by writing the Preface. Similarly, I am grateful to Dr. Rajbali Pande, Head of Department of Ancient Indian History and Culture at Jabalpur University, for his valuable Review and suggestion to me to include two chapters in the book, viz., '*Stree Dhana* and Succession' and 'Comparative Position of Indian Woman in World Civilizations'.

I have added the chapter on 'Woman in Indian Sculpture' on the suggestion of my eldest son, Chandra Chur Mani, Associate Editor, 'Hindi Encyclopaedia.' He has selected and suitably included pictures relating to Indian Art and Archaeology in the book, has prepared the Bibliography, carried out proof reading and in a way, edited the book.

I am especially grateful to the A.S.I. New Delhi, D.B. Taraporevala Sons and Co. Pvt. Ltd., Bombay, Dr. Benjamin Rolland, U.S.A. and Cambridge University Press, London for the Illustrations appearing in the book.

Chandra Bali Tripathi

1
Essentials of Indian Culture

Indian culture is widely acclaimed for the unique hold that *dharma* has been exercising over normal social behavior and the way it has been successful in preserving its identity in the maze of bewildering heterogeneity. It is basically different from other world cultures in this respect. Though it is not possible to give an exact definition of Indian culture, its distinguishing feature has been to curb the brute in man, bring out his divinity and help him in realizing God. Presence of animal instincts in man is natural, there being many things in common; like, eating, sleeping, fear and fornication. It is not possible to eradicate these animal instincts, but their control is certainly possible. The thinkers in our society, while laying down principles of social behavior, had certainly kept this basic fact in mind. The greatest organiser of Indian society, Manu, declares that these instincts are natural to all living beings[1]. The *Mahabharata*, too, lays stress on the same fact, while stating, 'the tenets of *dharma* have been laid down to distinguish humans from animals and to lift the humans from the animal state.'[2] *Shrimad Bhagavata* says that in this world nobody needs to be told to indulge in fornication and to eat meats and to drink; these are natural to humans. It is only to keep these tendencies within limits that the institutions of marriage, Soma Yaga and Sautramani Yajna respectively have been evolved, though abstinence is more desirable.[3] This can be better explained by saying that the man comes to the world with inborn instincts of *artha* (desire for wealth) and *kama* (sexuality). As far as other creatures are concerned, nature herself controls and limits these instincts and they can not transgress these. But armed with the unique asset of intellect, the man is capable of moulding *artha* and *kama* in innumerable ways and keeping these within limits, if he so desires. And whereas other creatures have their rut according to laws of nature, man priding himself to be the Master of Nature can go to any limits of sensuality.

Many prehistoric communities have disappeared from the face of the earth due to unregulated sexual behaviour. Even in this age of civilization there are tribes that have not risen beyond this state. But the civilized man, endowed as he is with intellect and consciousness, can certainly not remain satisfied with this state of affairs. His intellect works towards need for preservation of the self and his clan, enjoyment of happiness, amassing of wealth and resources, and continuous development of these natural instincts. His desires keep on growing and he develops his intellectual prowess to the utmost limit in inventing objects of pleasure to satisfy these desires.

The level of enjoyment of unregulated pleasures is the *asuri* level. Those who believe that there is no power that controls this universe, that it has no creator, maintainer and destroyer and that there are no inviolable rules regulating this universe, hold that the ultimate purpose of their life is to direct whatever the world offers towards mechanical fulfilment of their earthly desires. The *Gita* calls persons with this ideology *asuras*.[4] We can not say that India did not have people with such line of thought. Charvaka was the propagator of this line of thinking, whose belief was that eating, drinking and making merry was the highest goal in life. But Charvaka philosophy could not establish itself as a serious system and could never become a part of Indian culture. It is another matter how it was received in the Hedonism of Western philosophy.

Culture has its beginnings when the man rises above this situation and realizes that he cannot enjoy his *artha* and *kama* as he likes. There is the whole world around him and as the *artha* and *kama* desires and efforts of all and sundry clash with one another, his *artha* and *kama* are in perennial jeopardy, resulting in a sort of compromise between self-interest and interests of others. With a view to curb uncontrolled desires, rules are framed for regulating the same and life thus gets fettered by restrictions. The relationship between the individual and the society gets regulated by reason, and with the resultant balance the society attains stability. Peace in sociey replaces squabbles, bickerings, antagonism and unhealthy struggles. Otherwise, violence would prevail, the society would be in constant turmoil and peace and happiness, which are ever cherished by mankind, would be a pipe dream. Lord Krishna lays down rules for avoiding disruption of society as essentials of *dharma*.[5] Many powerful nations in the world have disappeared due to non-adherence to tenets of *dharma*, which have a stabilizing effect on society.

All cultures are more or less similar so far as *artha* and *kama* are concerned. Only when we transcend these, we reach the third and higher stage, *dharma*, and this is an inseparable part of our culture. It has its roots in the conviction that there is an Almighty, All-pervading, All-conscious God who is responsible for creation and destruction of the universe, and without whose will nothing moves. He resides as the innermost Self in all beings and directs the universe with machine-like precision through His unimaginable Power, also known as His *lila* (sport) or *maya* (illusion).[6] The rules governing the society are also subject to this *Shakti* (power). However, the same *Shakti* has endowed Man with ability to develop, to rise to greatest heights and realize the Self.[7] The hallmark of this culture is that the Man reaps the fruits—good or bad—of all his good or bad deeds. Related with this is the unquestioned belief that the present life is not the end in the string of lives, that the man is born again and again to reap the fruits of his past deeds and that in this he has no choice. All the same, he is endowed with an ability to get rid of this helplessness and to free himself from the cycle of births and deaths and fruits of *karma* through appropriate means. All schools of Indian philosophy, including Buddhism and Jainism, subscribe to the Theory of *karma* and Rebirth. There is no doubt that these principles are an inseparable part of our culture and that these have got enshrined in the beliefs of adherents to all indigenous religions. Here we must clear the doubts created by Western thought regarding Cause and Effect of *karma* and Rebirth. According to them, such beliefs have a depressing effect on life, which becomes miserable, inert and lack-lustre. This is not so. At the root of this belief lies the fact that once you are sanguine that bad results of evil deeds follow you not only in this life, but in future lives as well, you will strive to do good. You derive consolation in the hope that the present may be miserable, but good deeds will open the doors to happiness in future, if not in this life, sure enough in future ones.

The saying of the wise that death can catch up with you anytime, and therefore, you must always follow the path of *dharma,* inspires you to do good deeds. It becomes your second nature to strive to make your life active, alert and meaningful, avoiding sin. These principles inspire you to strive hard, and figuratively speaking, feel yourself able, with God's Grace, to lift the universe like a ball! The lives of great men in history corroborate this. This God- made institution of *kala* (Time) and *karma* is the crux of Indian culture, wherein it is believed that the whole world is directed by a moral code, that it derives its existence from the Almighty God, that life is but a *dharma yajna* and that every living being propitiates The Almighty with his good deeds. A person brought up under this culture does not vivisect life in different spheres, like rooms in a house. He views life in totality and *dharma* is his only criterion, under all circumstances. In other words, he governs his actions in different spheres, like politics, trade, labour etc., according to principles of *dharma*.

The vision of culture does not end here. There is provision of *artha* and *kama*, though restrained by *dharma*. The involvement of *dharma* helps in exalting life by making it active, philanthropic and great. In fact, our culture goes a step further. Suppose you are able to master worldly pleasures and prosperity, and through *yajna*, charities (*dana*), austerities (*tapas*) are able to realize heavenly pleasures and happiness. Even so, this is not the ultimate and most desirable aim of life, because the real Self is not this body. That is *atman*, which transcends Senses, *manas*, and Intellect.[8] It is unaffected by pleasure and pain and all the disabilities in the world and is untouched by the three *gunas – sattva, rajas* and *tamas*, these *gunas* and *vikaras* being functions of *prakriti* (creation) and not *purusha* (creator). Pleasures and prosperity, both temporal and heavenly, are transient. There is undisputed cycle of happiness and pain; rather, as Maharshi Vyasa has said – 'there is more misery in the world than happiness.'[9] Further, by virtue of *yajnas* and righteous deeds the blessed ones attain divine worlds, like Indraloka etc. But the moment the accumulated *punya* ceases, they are dropped down on the earth.[10]

"The man wants to live for happiness. Is it only a mirage after which man has been wandering in vain since the beginning of life? The soul-science (*adhyatma*) says – No! Verily, it is the object of its search! Man, in his purest form, is inseparable from *atman* which has no trace of misery. In it there is no happiness in the worldly sense, but there is the Ultimate Happiness, which is perceptible to Intellect, but not to the senses. It is that Happiness, whose realization leaves nothing further to be desired."[11] This *atmananda* (happiness of the soul) is certainly within the reach of Man.

Once man realizes that the happiness after which he is hankering is not-real, but only a mirage, and once he experiences the real nature of *atman* and its inseparability from him, he becomes entitled to eternal happiness. This is *atmabodha* (self-realization), after which the search of God (*Paramatman*) ceases. This *atmabodha* is a subject of soul-science or Metaphysics. In the *Manusmriti* and the *Mahabharata* it is also known as *mokshadharma,* because it mainly embodies measures for freeing oneself from the shackles of old age, death and rebirth. India is often known as a country of spiritualists. It does not mean that in India all the people at all times have been engrossed in the search of soul. But it is certainly true that in the hoary past our sages (*rishis*) had realized the transient nature of worldly pleasures and prosperity and had devoted their entire lives in quest of the Eternal and *moksha* and realization thereof. The result of this tremendous effort was that spiritualism left an indelible mark on our culture.

Our oldest history is the *Rigveda,* which contains the famous *Nasadiya Sukta*. According to Lokamanya Tilak, mankind has not gone beyond the all- pervasive Truth, which the *rishi* of that *sukta* had realized with his spiritual vision.[12] In the physical world we come across numerous forms and denominations that are short-lived and are rooted in disunity. But the rishis, with their inward direct experience, had realized that underlying these is an element that permeates the entire universe.[13] Even though that basic element is indivisible, it appears to be in parts in this world comprising of myriads of forms and denominations and the indestructible Brahma permeates all the earthly objects that are continuously disintegrating.[14] The light that we get from the sun, moon, stars and fire etc. is all derived from that eternal Light which is the Light of all lights.[15] We cannot see that Light with the naked eye—not even with the most powerful instruments. If at all it can be compared, it is with the combined *tejas* (light) of thousands of suns.[16]

This ultimate Element is infinite—without a beginning, middle or end. It has permeated the entire universe with a mere fraction of Itself.[17] This truth is indescribable and beyond the scope of senses. It is beyond sound, touch, form, taste, and smell (*shabda, sparsha, rupa, rasa, gandha*).[18] It is beyond the reach of *manas* and its actual nature cannot be described by speech.[19] Even the choicest attributes in human language are unable to describe it fully. That is why '*Neti*' has been said about it, 'i.e., It is not this'—which is at best a negative definition.

The *rishis* from their practised knowledge have announced that all this is *Brahman*[20], that whatever there is, is but one, that nothing with many or even infinite names is real, that one who sees diversity embraces only death and that such a person can never free himself from the bondage of birth and death.[21] These visionaries had a direct realization that the *jivatma* is only a part of the *Paramatma*,[22] and that once the cover of ignorance is removed, the distinction between the two disappears. The *jivatma* then becomes one with *Brahman* and in this blessed state it starts visualizing itself in all the living beings and all living beings in itself.[23] This state is known as '*Brahmi Sthiti*' or '*Brahma nirvana*', which houses immortality.[24] It is that eternal happiness which the man hankers after, but is unable to achieve due to his pursuit of false pleasures and remains like a bird in the cage. The '*Nirvana*' which was attained by the Buddha was no different from this '*Brahma Nirvana*'.

The fulfilment of life's aim is said to lie in the quest of *Brahma* and the realization thereof, though a question is raised at times as to whether it is possible that the human beings as a whole, by transgressing the physical worldly shackles, could attain the '*Paramatma bhava*' or the Ultimate and experience the same within. Ideally speaking, even though plausible in theory, the concept is not only difficult, but according to Sri Aurobindo, it is hard to achieve as well. According to him, the man as a whole is barely uplifting himself and that nine-tenths of the human race is still in an uncivilized state.[25]

The *Brahma vidya,* which has its roots in the *Rigveda,* saw its development in the *Upanishads.* It got more clearly defined in the *Mahabharata* (*Gita*), *Brahmasutras,* the Commentaries (*Bhashyas*) of the *acharyas* and the vast Sanskrit literature. The regional languages also had the benefit of this knowledge from time to time. From the Himalayas to the Kanyakumari and from the eastern to the western seas the saints, holy men and siddhas have kept the torch of this knowledge burning brightly through their personalities and their *abhangas, vachanas* and *banis* (teachings in verses). The result has been that whereas the world has remained engrossed in materialism elsewhere, the symbols of this tradition even in recent times like, Ramakrisna Paramahamsa, Ramana Maharsi, Mahatma Gandhi, Yogi Aurobindo have shown the path of light to the humanity groping in the dark. That which exists can never be totally destroyed,[26] and that the creation, which is the outward manifestation of *prakriti,* though not independent, is infinite[27] are the principles accepting which the man strives for *moksha.* But the realization of *moksha* is extremely difficult. It is like walking on the sharp edge of a knife.[28] Only one out of thousands tries to achieve this and not even one out of these strugglers achieves complete knowledge. Or may be, he attains God after trying in many births.[29] This is what is called '*shreyas*'. Anything that is attainable outside this is '*preyas*'. The greatest inspiration and contribution of our culture is that the man should strive for '*shreyas*' in preference to '*preyas*'.[30]

In the olden days all human endeavour was classified into four parts known as '*purusharthas*'. The seeds of this idea are found in the *Rigveda.* These *purusharthas* have been detailed in practically all the philosophies, *Dharmashastras, Itihasas* (histories), *Mahakavyas* (*Mahabharata* and

Ramayana), *Smritis* and *Puranas*. Even the fine arts find a place in this. The science of *moksha* rose to great heights, yet it did not hamper physical progress. Meaningful researches were carried out in Arts and Sciences; like, Ayurveda, Dhanurveda, weaponry, chemistry, astronomy, mathematics, poetry, drama, etc., which went to raise the standard of living. Architecture, crafts, music etc. brought about finesse. *artha* and *kama* were always considered desirable, and it was stressed that there should be no clash with *dharma* and *moksha*, at the same time ensuring that there was no exclusive pursuit of the former. It is in this context that the *Smriti* says that the desires do not get satiated by objects of desire, these only grow further, just as the fire burns brighter with the *havish*.[31] In order that life might not become aimless, *dharma* was ordained to control *artha* and *kama* and *moksh* was considered the ultimate goal.

Many schools of thought have sprung up from time to time in regard to institution of *ashramas* and at times some of these appear to be contradictory. But an analysis reveals that these are all basically related to the same concept of '*nihshreyasa*' or *moksha*. Where, on the one hand *sanyasa* and Renunciation were given the pride of place, on the other, the doors of *moksha* were considered open for the householder engaged in worldly chores, as well. It was ordained that the wise person could attain *moksha* by engaging himself in acts of goodness for the humanity without any attachment and without a thought of the good or bad results of his actions.

The sages established *sanyas, karmayoga* and *jnanayoga* amongst the above two ways of life—*nivritti* and *pravritti*. In the former, need for complete renunciation of *karma*, and in the latter the need for constant engagement in desirable *karmas* for the good of society, even after attaining the heights of *jnana* or knowledge, were emphasized. The former was called '*jnana nishtha*' and the latter, '*karma yoga*'.[32]

In the words of the author of *Purva Mimamsa*, Jaimini, we have concentrated on the process that brings about good for the humanity and at the same time helps in attainment of *moksha*. *Dharma* really means only this.[33] It has been so described by Vyasa—"It is essential to follow that *dharma* which is helpful in achievement of both *artha* and *kama*, but it is really strange that inspite of my vehement exposition nobody is prepared to listen to me."[34]

The concept of *chaturvarga* gave rise to the institution of four *ashramas*; viz., *brahmacharya*, *garhasthya*, *vanaprastha*, and *sanyasa*, and this had been established long before Vyasa. In the first *ashrama*, the body, *manas* and intellect are developed and purified as a preparation for the second one. In the second *ashama* enjoyment of *artha* and *kama* in a righteous manner and discharging of one's duty towards family, society and the nation are the essential features. In the *vanaprastha* it is ordained that the man should give up his home and hearth and spend his time in public service and thus prepare himself for *moksha*. It is only after self-realization that the wise can think of good for all humanity and that is the way of *sanyasa* or *karmatyaga*.

The knowledge of unity of *brahma* and *atman* is essential for both *sanyasa* and *karmayoga*. But the *jnana marga* is extremely tough.[35] Therefore, *bhakti marga* was evolved with a view to opening the doors of *moksha* for all and sundry, and it became an inseparable part of our culture in times to come. *bhakti*, ultimately, leads to complete *jnana*. The Lord has assured that those who worship him with unflinching and undivided devotion attain the *jnana* that leads to *moksha*.[36] The principles and the ultimate form of *bhakti* have remained the same throughout, but the variety of practices have led to branches and sub-branches.

A *mahamantra* that strikes at the root of all the controversy in the name of the religions and sects appears in the *Rigveda;* and that is—"God or *Sat* is one and the wise describe That one is various way".[37] This is at the root of various methods of worship or *bhakti*. Starting from the invocation of the Transcendent, and going on to the same for the subtle *manas* and then *prana* etc., worship of the human incarnation of the Almighty ensued. The underlying principle in the *jnana* and *bhakti margas* and their subsequent forms has been that inclinations of people differ and that their moral and intellectual levels are also at varying stages of development; and therefore, distinction has to be made between what is good and suitable for each of them. The *Mundakopanishad* summarises this idea as follows:

"Just as rivers flowing in all directions disappear in the sea and they lose their identity, similarly the wise differing though they do in their inclinations and attainments, ultimately dissolve into the one Effulgent Truth that is God, who is nameless and formless."[38]

References

1. Manu, 5.56.
2. Mahabharata Shanti Parva, 294, 29.
3. Bhagavata 11.5.11.
4. Gita, 16.8.
5. Mahabharata Karna Parva, 69.57-58.
6. Gita, 8.61.
7. Gita, 6.5.
8. Gita, 3.42; Kath Up. 1.3; 10-11.
9. Mahabharata Shanti Parva, 205, 6; 330, 16.
10. Gita, 9.21-22.
11. Gita, 6, 21-22.
12. Lokamanya Bal Gangadhar Tilak: Gita Rahasya p. 258.
13. Ishavasyopanishad 1, Gita 7, 7; 9.4.
14. Gita, 13, 16.27.
15. Mundakopanishad 2.2,9.10.
16. Gita, 11.12.

17. Gita, 15.3, 11.42.
18. Katha, Up. 1.3.15.
19. Tattaiyopanishad, Brahmananda Valli 2.
20. Chhandogya 3.13.14.
21. Brih. 3.14; Katha 2.1,11.
22. Gita, 15.7.
23. Isha. 6.7; Gita 6.29.
24. Gita 2, 72; 5.
25. Sri Aurobindo: The Foundation of Indian Culture.
26. Gita, 2.16.
27. Gita, 13.14.
28. Kathopanishad, 1.2.2.
29. Gita, 7.3; 7.19.
30. Kathopanishad, 1.2.2.
31. Manu, 2.94.
32. Gita 3.3.
33. Vaisheshika Sutra.
34. Mahabharata Svargarohana Parva, 5.62.
35. Gita 12.5.
36. Gita 10.10.
37. Rigveda, 1.164.46.
38. Mundakopanishad 3.2.8.

2

Man and Woman in the Social Development Cycle

In certain societies it was held that women do not have souls. But in India it was the belief that it was the same soul in woman as in man and that she was equally entitled to realize it. That is why it has been said in the Gita that 'devotion to God can lead women, Shudras and the lowest of the lowlies to salvation'.[1] It goes to establish that since the same soul exists in men and women, both are basically one.

In confirmation of this theory the Vedic literature lays down that the *Purusha* (Cosmic Being) is very close to *Prajapati*.[2] Not only that, *Purusha* is *Prajapati* Himself.[3] Here we must understand that *Purusha* includes woman. The atheists believe that the universe is a function of nature and that there is no Creator element.[4] Opposed to this is the Vedic belief that All-conscious God is the creator, maintainer and destroyer of the universe and that the existence of the latter depends upon that of the former. It is stated in the *Subalopanishad* that in the beginning of creation the Prajapati created man from His one half, and woman from the other. The *Brihadaranyaka Upanishad* also propounds that the One Almighty desired to become Two and He became as if man and woman were joined together. He separated this form of His and man and wife were born.[5]

This concept of the *Upanisads* found acceptance in the *Dhamashastras* and *Puranas* as well. The *Manusmriti* describes the process of Creation at length and propounds that Hiranyagarbha divided Himself into two and created man and woman from each part.[6] He became Two out of His own volition, creating man form from the right part and woman form from the left; and He did this through yoga or His Divine power of Creation.[7] Thus the concept of oneness of man and woman as propounded in the *Devi Bhagavata* gained acceptance among thinkers. All the foregoing concepts were subsequently compounded, so to say, in the Valmikiya Ramayana. This priceless literary piece of our culture, while delineating the difference between man and woman lays down that the crux of the *Shastras* and *Vedas* is that basically woman is no different from man.[8]

In later times the philosopher poet, Kalidasa, incorporated in his poetry the desire of the Creator to divide Himself into man and woman with a view to extend His creation.[9] In line with this concept he has held Parvati and Parameshwara as the prime cause of the universe and worshipped Them as such in the beginning of his book, Raghuvamsha.[10] The concept of Ardhanarishwara is also based on the same concept. The provision of the wife being seated to the left of the husband in the performance of religious rites is also based on the principle that woman was created from the left half of the Almighty, which gives her the name *vamangana*.

The basic identity of man and woman as outlined in the theory of Creation finds corroboration in standard literature and in the lives of great men. Acceptance of the theory that both man and woman were created from equal parts of the same Consciousness takes us to important conclusions. Indian philosophy looks for unity in diversity and inspires us to become one with that Entity. Its speciality is that it pinpoints oneness in the diverse forms of nature, and the one and only unique Formless Shakti that permeates those diverse forms. Their contact should, therefore, be encouraging harmony and not opposition. That is why man and woman have been compared to two wheels of a chariot and it has been emphasized that the destination can be reached promptly only when the two wheels run in co-ordination. It is also patently incorrect and unjust to accuse the authors of *Dharmasutras* of partisanship in any way, because it is those very ancient thinkers who considered the whole world as one family. Those who harbour doubts are either immature or their resentment is born out of frustration and shortsightedness inherent in modern materialistic thinking. This only encourages family feuds and class struggle in society. How far removed this situation is from our ideal that teaches us to enlist the support of even gods in heaven in guiding our behaviour! [11]

But the symbolic unity of man and woman does not mean that all their behaviours will be identical. They are obviously different from the point of view of body-structure and sex.

Due to these special features their fields of activity differ to a large extent. There are chores which can not be performed by a man as well as by a woman. Similarly, there are jobs in which the expertise of man is so obvious that there can not be two opinions. Thus the division of work between man and woman takes place in a natural way. This is known as their *samanya dharma* in our *Dharmashastras*. For example, activities of women are domestic; like, rearing a child and household chores. On the other hand, outdoor activities like; agriculture, military craft etc. are more suited to men. There are, of course exceptions to this general rule. History bears out that under special circumstances women have performed many tasks considered to be within the ambit of men most admirably. Further, it has been proved by scientific research that all the spheres of activity of men and women can not be identical. It will, therefore, not do to insist on rights and liberty in every matter. The thinking has to be job-oriented and without conflict. The compendium of behaviour (*Nitishastra*) does not lay down that we should be divorced from reason and that we should shut ourselves off from all new light. *Mahakavi* Kalidasa has rightly emphasized that nothing is good because it is old, nor is anything bad merely because it is new. A system must stand the test of reason.

References

1. Gita, 9.32.
2. Shatapathe Brahmana, 4.3.4.3.
3. Ibid, 6.2.1.23.
4. Gita, 16.8.
5. Brih. Up., 1.4.3.
6. Manu., 1.32.
7. Devi Bhagavata, 2.27.
8. Valmikiya Ramayana, Kishkindha Kanda 24.38.
9. Kumara Sambhava 2.7.
10. Raghuvamsha of Kalidasa, 1.1.
11. Gita, 3.10.11.

3

Relationship between Man and Woman: Principles of Reproduction

The relationship between husband and wife, established through marriage, is a religious bond. Its basis is a great ideal. It is not the result of an Agreement or Contract as in many other cultures. In this ideal the underlying concept is not satiation of sex, but performance of a socio-religious duty. This has been enunciated in *Apastamba Dharmadhikarana*, which lays down that the relationship between husband and wife is governed by *dharma*.[1] The basis for this statement is the Rigveda. During marriage the husband addresses his wife thus: "I am marrying you for good fortune. May we live together till death doth us part! Gods Bhaga, Aryama, Savita and Purandhri have given you to me in order that I may perform my duties as the Master of the House."[2] *Atharva Veda* also says the same thing. Here, too, the husband tells his wife, "The gods have given you to me to enable me to perform my duties as *grihapati*. You follow the duties of a wife according to *dharma* and I shall do the same as your *prajapati* (father of your would be children)."[3] Similarly, according to Manu, at the time of *prajapatya* marriage, which is the best of all marriage systems, the father of the bride addresses the newly-weds thus," Both of you perform together according to *dharma*."[4]

In regard to relationship between husband and wife, the Vedic thought holds that in the performance of *yajna*-

based *Vedic* rites both have equal rights. In olden days setting up of the sacred fire—*garhapatyagni* was a must. The ritual fire before which marriage is performed was brought by the husband along with the wife and set up in his house. It was the duty of the wife to keep it burning life long. The wife would use the same for cooking and the husband and the wife would together perform the '*agnihotra*' morning and evening. The husband and the wife were to offer *havish* to gods together. (*havish* is the matter fed to this *garhapatyagni* as offering to gods.)[5] Keeping in view this joint activity of husband and wife, the Smriti lays down functions of reproduction for the wife and the husband. According to Shruti, the two together embark upon the path of *dharma*.[6]

This relationship has been compared to a chariot and it has been said that the husband and wife are the two horses driving the chariot and that the chariot can ply only when the two are properly yoked together.[7]

This concept has been very clearly expanded in the later literature as gleaned through histories, *Dharmashastras* and the Epics. When Manu insisted upon implicit faithfulness for the wife, irrespective of the fact that the husband might be virtueless, a debauch or devoid of qualities, and laid down that the wife must serve him like a god,[8] he did not grant licence to the husband. On the contrary, Manusmriti and the Mahabharata declare that the husband must not merely support the wife, but respect her as well. These further declare that where women are worshipped, gods dwell. Where they are not respected, prosperity disappears and the lineage gradually gets extinguished. The woman that enjoys security and respect in life is verily blessed.[9] The exhortation of sage Kanva to Shakuntala to earn respect of her husband[10] establishes this fact, which has not only a moral sanctity, but is seen to be a fact as well.

Relationship between Man and Woman

In the vedic religion it is essential to be with a wife, and no religious rites could be performed without one. The *Taittiriya Brahmana* lays down that a man has no right to perform *yajnas* if he has no wife.[11] It appears Panini has fixed the root of the word *patni* in his *Ashtadhyayi* as "one who assists the husband in *yajna*."[12] In the Atharvaveda (5.7.36) the husband speaks to the wife thus. "Let our eyes be full of honey and our mouths with oil. Establish me in your heart." This feeling of oneness of thought and marital closeness sweatens the relationship between man and woman and is unique in the annals of world literature. Though the emotion of love was predominant in this concept, its practice was not based on sexuality, but on procreation according to dictates of *dharma* (*dharmartha prajotpatti*). Amongst the accepted ideals prevalent in the post-vedic era, which was specially connected with Ikshvaku dynasty rulers, Kalidasa has described marriage to be meant for progeny.[13] In the *Valmikiya Ramayana* it has been described that when, during marriage, Rama was facing Agni, King Janaka told him,"My daughter, Sita, is now your partner. Accept her. Let her follow you like a shadow, be a harbinger of good fortune and remain ever faithful to you." So saying the King sprinkled *mantra*-blessed water.[14] The direction in the Taittiriya Brahmana that a person without a wife is not entitled to perform *yajna* and the principle outlined in the *Ramayana* of complete partnership find full corroboration in the character of Rama. The fact that Rama kept a gold statue of Sita by his side while performing *yajna* during the exile of Sita, does not only denote his faith in monogamy, but his commitment to the above direction. The custom of annointing the Queen as well at the time of coronation of a King was vedic in origin. The seating of Sita beside Rama and that of Draupadi beside Yudhisthira at the time of coronation are historical events that serve to highlight the sanctity of relationship between man and woman. It is significant that this ideal is maintained even today in Hindu society.

In the *Taittiriya Brahmana* the wife is called *ardhangini* (half-body) of the husband, and the concept has been totally imbibed in our culture. Where in *Shatapatha Brahmana* (5.2.1.10) the man is said to be incomplete without the wife, it only means that the man should try to achieve self-realization with the pursuit of *dharma* alongwith his wife.

It is amazing that certain concepts regarding procreation appearing in the *Rigveda* tally with the modern Law of Eugenics. The *Rigveda* (5.3.4.34) states that the wife is the abode of the husband. The same thing has been stated in the *Vajasaneya Brahmana* thus that the man is only half the soul till he takes a wife and begets a child. That is why the knowledgeable say that the *bharta* (husband) is the same as *bharya* (wife)[15].

The above concept appears in the Manusmriti thus: "The man becomes complete with the conjunction of these three—self, wife and progeny. The one who is *bharta* is himself *bharya* or *angana*."[16] From this concept *Manusmriti* went on further to propound that "we do know that the Almighty (Prajapati) has ordained that even by renunciation the relationship of *bharta* and *bharya* does not snap."[17] In the eyes of Valmiki the non-duality of husband and wife is the crux of the Vedas. He has expressed himself that from the *shastras* and *Vedas* it is clear that the wife is inseparable from the husband and that no offering (*dana*) is higher than the *kanyadana* (giving away a daughter in marriage).[18] In this connection the *Smriti* talks of rebirth of the Atman in the form of a son. The essence of all these theories, however, is the importance of continuity of the race. The Vedas are not said to be compendium of knowledge for nothing. The idea of continuity of race propounded by the *rishis* in the hoary past has been corroborated by modern genetics, too. Prof. Julian S Huxley has similar views. [19]

References

1. Ap. 2.13.12.
2. Rigveda 10.85.36.
3. Atharvaveda, 14.1.50-51.
4. Manu, 3.30.
5. Rigveda 5.1.173.2.
6. Manu, 9.96.
7. Rigveda, 8.33.18.
8. Manu, 5.154.
9. Mahabharata, Anushasana , 46.5.9.15; Manusmiti, 3.57-58.
10. Shakuntalam of Kalidasa 7.29.
11. Tattariya Brahmana.
12. Ashtadhyayi of Panini 4.1.33.
13. Raghuvansha of Kalidasa, 1.7.
14. Val. Ram. Ayodhya Kanda 73,32-33-34.
15. Vajasaneya Brahmana.
16. Manusmiti, 9.45.
17. Manusmiti, 9.46.
18. Val. Ram. Kishkindha Kanda 24.38.
19. Prof. Julian S. Huxley: The Streams of Life, London 1929.

4
The Position of Women in Society

The tradition of visualizing women as different forms of the Primordial Power (Shakti) is very old in our religious texts. The entire temporal or vedic literature from Rigveda down has depicted woman in keeping with her greatness born out of her dutiful living, sacrifice and like qualities. Her honourable position as mother has not been so merely as a theme of literature, but we find her so in day-to-day social interaction as well. Even in the language of day-to-day business, women were called *devis*, but men were never addressed as *devas*. Later on, certain rules were framed keeping in view special convenience of men, but disregard of women was never intended. This most probably must have happened due to certain special circumstances and requirements. It is, therefore, not justified to brand men as selfish or dictatorial. Women have always been held in respect in our society.

In ancient literature women have been looked upon as forms of goddesses on account of their proficiency in arts and science,[1] and the *Dharmashastras* have considered them *avadhya* (literally, never to be killed). That women could not be killed under any circumstance had become a dictum right in the beginning of organized society. In the Shatapatha Brahmana[2] woman has been adorned with the epithet '*Shri*', which establishes her grandeur. In fact, all the forms of the Goddess find their origin in the woman. She has been described as the embodiment of knowledge and prowess, giver of charities (*dana*), unending peace and prosperity and provider of food for all.

In the *Mahabharata* the *riju* (pious) women desirous of good for their husbands have been called '*lokamatas*' and it has been said that the earth remains full of vegetation and grains on their account.[3] A kingly rule that could not remove woes of women was considered a failure. In regard to status of ideal women the *Chhandogya Upanisad* mentions Ashvapati, the ruler of Kekaya, who boasted that his kingdom had not one woman of loose character.[4] It also highlights that in order to prevent loss of character amongst women, it was the duty of the State to prevent immorality among men as well. Similarly, Buddha once explained the stability of the kingdom of Vajjis as due to rigid laws for prevention of the crime of rape. When Magadha King, Ajatashatru, sought his advice before invading the Vajjis, the Buddha told him that so long as the Vajjis stuck to their seven qualities, they were invincible. One of these was that the Vajjis never applied force on women.

Laws existed for ensuring welfare of women. An ideal implementation of these laws is noticed in the dictum of the *Ramayana* that a nation which looked after the welfare of its women was a happy one and that if they were in misery, such a nation deserved strong condemnation. [5] That women could never be killed is established from the fact that even Lord Rama had faced a doubt in his mind at the time when he was to kill the *rakshasi*, Tadaka, in the hermitage of sage Vishwamittra and that a solution was found after great deliberation.[6] In the Mahabharata in the story of the demon Baka a woman emphasizes as to how even *asura* women were not to be slain, because even the demons knew the tenets of *dharma*.[7] This appears in the story of a Brahmana family of Ekachakra which was to become food for Baka. Similarly, there is the incident of Hanumana not killing Lankini, who was stopping his progress, but only leaving her unconscious. There are many such examples.

The *Manusmriti* lays down drastic punishment for killers of women. According to this, there should be capital punishment for those engaged in misrule in the name of the king, those spreading revolt, those killing women, children and Brahmanas and those in collusion with the enemies of the nation. In the *Panchatantra*, which has established ideals of politics and sociology in the form of stories, killing of women has been held to be a sin, their protection bringing heavenly reward. In those days it was an ordinary custom that women were allowed to move out of a crowd or on the road first.[8] It was also considered a duty to help a woman in distress during a journey. It is seen that at places women were exempted from ghat-tax. It was the duty of the state to ensure security and welfare of women who had no guardians. Similarly, women were let off with minor punishment even for heinous crimes. The seemingly lax rules and preferential treatment in administration for women were, however, based on practical considerations. These were: weaker constitution, helplessness in certain circumstances, reduced ability to carry important social burdens and their respected status.[9]

In regard to the honoured position of women *mahakavi* Bhavabhuti says in the exhortation of the self- realized *karmayogi*, like Janaka, to Sita in Uttara Ramacharita, thus: "It is not material whether you are my daughter or pupil. Your conduct has reached the zenith, which has generated special respect in me for you. Inspite of being a woman and of young age, you deserve to be worshipped by the world, because the talented are respected on account of their talent, and not on account of their age or sex."[10]

Similarly Janaka, while felicitating Arundhati, wife of sage Vasishtha, and calling her '*jagadvandya*' and a *devi* like Usha, has, in fact, honoured the whole lot of women who are symbols of prosperity and harbingers of righteous progress.[11] The later *acharyas* have also honoured the women generously. The appointment of Bharati as an arbitrator in the *shastric* debate between Shankaracharya and Mandana Mishra is an excellent example of honouring the women. Bhaskara II, has similarly furthered the same idea by naming the priceless book on Mathematics as Lilavati after the name of his talented daughter. Similarly, the greatest exponent of Vedanta in his time, Vachaspati Mishra (9th. cen. A.D.) has named his commentary (*tika*) *Bhamati*, on the *Shankara Bhashya* (commentary on the *Brahma Sutras*) after his learned wife and has thus expressed his respect for women as a whole.

The vedic and temporal literature do not merely eulogize the women while determining their status in society. There are several instances when women have been severely criticized as well. But due to lack of a balanced view, some people unfamiliar with Sanskrit language and its tradition, have expressed their narrow views targetting only Goswami Tulasidasa. Here it must be clarified that it is not fair to criticize seemingly disrespectful utterances in regard to women without reference to the context and the thinking of the characters. It has been said in the *Shatapatha Brahmana*, "Women are fond of trivialities. So they pick up friendship very fast among those engaged in music and dance."[12] *Maitrayani Samhita* also states that women are liars and unfaithful.[13]

Even the *Rigveda* is sometimes highly critical of them—'they are not real friends and their hearts are like those of wolves.'[14] This criticism comes from Pururava, whom Urvashi forsook and left for heaven. Pururava calls her a wolf out of extreme indignation. Similarly the *mantra* of the *Maitrayani Samhita* criticizing the women refers only to characterless women. Therefore, it is baeless to hold disrespect to the women as a class based on these statements. The *Vedic mantras* are resplendent with praise of women, the homage to Usha being a case in point.

Whereas there is praise in the *Manusmriti* for honest women, on the basis of *Vedic* thought it has been stated for the unfaithful thus—"Neither she worries about good features, nor age, nor handsomeness of the man, nor his ugliness. Due to her natural instinct for sex and being devoid of love by nature, she acts in defiance of her husband."[15] Puranas and the *Mahabharata* also contain some such thoughts;[16] but we must not treat those as a final verdict on the nature and characteristics of women. Similarly when Goswami Tulasidasa says "those women who remain chaste due to lack of opportunity or due to fear", he does not refer to all women. Again, Goswamiji has placed a drum, uneducated person, animal, Shudra and woman as deserving torture. But it is in a specific context and should not be taken to cover women etc. as a class. Coming as it does from a disciplinarian recluse like Goswamiji, whose vision was to establish an ideal society, it deserves to be ignored. There is no doubt that Tulasi and Kabir were one in castigating the society in order to keep it trim. That seems to be the secret behind their unorthodox statements. In the *Valmikiya Ramayana* the poet, while referring to the selfishness of Kaikeyi, has clarified that all women are not so.[17] No doubt, those writers who have enumerated only the shortcomings of the women were limited and narrow in their outlook. The usual human weaknesses are common to men and women. Therefore, no one is entitled to be called a person of character on the basis of decrying women, nor is woman hating a right step towards establishment of rules of conduct.

Some thinkers laid so much stress on controlling sexual activity and thought that it did not always had a healthy effect on large sections of society and the distinction between sublimation of thought on the one hand and ungenerous attitude towards women in the context of controlling sexuality became blurred. They even deprecated *pravritti marga* (the way of a house-holder), for which it became imperative to decry all women along with enjoyment of objects of pleasure and riches. Varahamihira (505-97 A.D.) has condemned such thinkers. According to him, those who see only shortcomings in women and no plus points are bad people and their sayings are full of ill will.[18] Varahamihira was a realist. He could not tolerate woman baiting. Castigating such thinkers he says, "The scriptures have laid down that neither woman should disregard man, nor man, his wife. But if the husband does not bother, the wife is the better of the two. Satiation of sexual desire is not possible even in a hundred years. A man gets out of it only when he starts losing his energy. On the other hand, women are stable and generally shy away from sin. When alone, the man makes efforts to please the woman, but she keeps these a secret. On the other hand, wicked men defame sinless women."[19] Bhavabhuti has also expressed himself similarly. He says those who criticize the excellence of great writings for no rhyme or reason are like the wicked woman-haters.[20]

For controlling sexuality the scriptures of the *yogamargis* as well as certain doctrines of Buddhists, Jains and Siddhas have denounced the women at length. For the same purpose *Manusmiti*, however, instead of decrying the woman, lays down that a person should avoid sitting alone even with his sister or daughter. He reasons it out by saying that 'the senses are so strong that these overpower even the wise.'[21] A Chinese writer, in order to avoid woman hating, has taken the plea: 'When we consider that nobody has come into the world without his mother, our thinking becomes liberal and we dare not decry all women.'[22] Most probably the idea has been borrowed from the statement of Mahatma Gandhi that a woman becomes reassured regarding her character after becoming a mother. Gandhiji was himself a follower of the dictum—which is the hallmark of the thinking of leaders of society in regard to position of women. As a matter of fact, in literature wherever the vices of women have been enumerated, the same has been done for men as well. An example appears in the Prakrita portion of *Malavikagnimitra* wherein Queen Iravati, noticing the infatuation of King Agnimitra for Malavika, calls all men unfaithful and accuses them of breach of faith. She cites the example of the doe which drawn by the music of the hunter loses all sense and falls into his trap, and repents that she never knew that she would fall a prey to the guiles of the deceitful king.[23] Similarly, in the *Theri Gathas* of Buddhist literature the Theris have profusely decried bad men. The correct attitude, according to *shastras,* is one wherein baseless accusation is not acceptable either by men or women. In connection with controlling sexual desires, the Chinese traveller Itsing (later part of 7th. cen A. D.) in his record of travels through India makes a mention of the *bhikshu* (recluse) Rahulamitra of Nalanda who would not set his eye on any woman, barring his mother and sister. In the world full of desires, he had considered this step essential to control the senses and thus he had set an example of self-control. The religious teachings have ordained such self-control. There has never been an effort to decry man or woman as a class in regard to their general conduct or inherent nature.

The Daughter not an object of Neglect

In the context of social status of women it must be discussed whether the daughter has been considered undesirable in Indian culture. It will be but natural to look for the earliest references in the vedas. On the basis of a *mantra* in the *Atharvaveda,* which lays down how to change over a girl into a boy in the foetus, a writer has concluded that in those days a girl child was not desirable.[24] But that conclusion is erroneous. It depends upon personal needs and convenience whether a son or a daughter is desired. Therefore, merely because the *mantra* lays down how to change the sex of the foetus, it does not mean that girls were not welcome at all. The same author later goes on to quote a *mantra* in the *Rigveda* that *Dyava* and *Prithivi* are like two sisters and both are jewels of their parents.[25] This *mantra* even seems to laud the birth of two daughters. This is further corroborated by the statement that blessed is he who has several daughters.[26] The *mantra* of the Rigveda that 'the same pleasure which the father gets from a son is enjoyed by the mother from the daughter; rather much more,'[27] will, no doubt, put all doubts at rest. Even the philosophically oriented *Upanishads* carry the same vedic thought. The *Brihadaranyaka Upanishad* prescribes a recipe of eating *tila* and rice fried in ghee for begetting a learned and long-living daughter.[28] The provision of daughter's share in the patrimony (*daya*) is worth consideration. It ordains that 'the daughter should be considered like son', because just as the soul begets itself in the form of a son, it also gets born as a daughter.'[29] The *Mahabharata* permits only such a house-holder to take to *sanyasa* as has discharged all his obligations of a house-holder, which includes marrying off the daughters.[30]

It appears that the problem of marriage of daughters gave rise to situations leading to the imagined neglect of the girl-child. In this connection a statement appearing in the *Panchatantra* is usually quoted, viz., 'the birth of a daughter causes grave anxiety. The problem arises as to where to marry her. Even after marriage, will she be happy? Verily, to be father of a girl is a great sorrow.'[31] Dr. Altekar negates this theory by saying that the father of the girl gets engrossed in her bringing up and in trying to make her the best, and in doing so he has no time for unnecessary worries.[32] Dr. Rama Shankar Tripathi has also quoted this excerpt from the *Panchatantra*.[33] Dr. Altekar's assertion seems to express the social sentiment correctly. Even so, if we look at the context in the *Panchatantra* in which being father of a girl has been held to be woeful, it will appear to be an exaggeration. In the story, a king on learning of his unmarried daughter falling in the trap of a lecher, expresses his indignation thus: "Rivers and women have similar effects; their banks and families being similar. The rivers destroy their banks with their water and the women destroy their families by their misdeeds."[34] This is in keeping with the age-old Indian thinking in which the character of their women has been of constant concern. Viewed against this background, the outbursts of an indignant father decrying the birth of a daughter should not be taken literally. Anxiety regarding marriage and requirements of arranging dowry beyond means have been the subject matter of folk songs, too, which depict the miseries befalling a household with the birth of a daughter. In one Bhojpuri song the mother-in-law and the husband's sister are shown to be keeping the house dark on the birth of a daughter and the husband is depicted as not even talking to the wife decently. Later, when the talk of the girl's marriage takes place, they all wish that nobody should have a daughter. All this forces the girl's mother to lament that if she had known that a daughter was coming, causing all round misery, she would have aborted her by eating the bitter 'Mirichajharara'. In this folk-song the mother's anguish is not caused by lack of love for the girl-child; rather, this is indicative of the harmful outcome of the dowry system, with which our society has been plagued for centuries and which has given rise to many evils. Thus it will not be correct to conclude that in Indian society girls have been unwanted. In every age filial love has been the norm, in keeping with which King Janaka says in the *Ramayana*—"By marrying off Sita, who is dearer to me than my life, to Rama, I shall be absolved of my *virya shulka* (duty enjoined upon a father).[35] It has been an ancient belief in our society that the son protects father and forefathers on one side, and maternal grandfather on the other, from hell. But the example of Gandhari in the *Mahabharata*, where she desires to have a daughter even after having a hundred sons, is indicative of love for the girl-child. She was also of the view that the son of a daughter would protect her (Gandhari's) husband from hell.[36] This religious belief is present to this day in Hindu society. This belief was not limited only to the princely class in those days, but was there amongst the high and the low alike. The words of the poor Brahmana of Ekachakra in Mahabharata, who refused to accept the pleadings of his daughter to allow her to go to the demon Baka in order to save the family from extinction are sufficient to underline a father's love for his daughter and are also indicative of the general thinking in the society. When he says—"Some men love sons better and some, daughters; but for me both are equal", it is only a reflection of the views of the creator of the Mahabharata.[37] It is also seen that in those days those without sons had a special attachment for daughters. That is why Kunti was brought up with great affection not only by her father, Kuntibhoja, but relation, Shurasena, as well and the ruler of Manipura, Chitrangada, had given his all to his only daughter, Chitrangada.

An excellent example of filial affection is that of *maharshi* Kanva, who had forgotten all *atmajnana* while sending off his foster daughter, Shakuntala, to Dushyanta. He could not withhold his tears. He says, "Today Shakuntala will go away—this thought alone is disturbing a recluse like me". It can be imagined how difficult separation from the daughter is for ordinary householders![38] How important a daughter is in Indian society will also be established from the direction of the greatest exponent of the *shastras*, Vyasa, who has laid down that a major fruit of hearing the entire *Mahabharata* is the birth of a fortune bringing daughter.[39] Later, we shall also discuss the contribution of women, individually and as a class, in the growth of civilization.

References

1. Durga Saptashati,l 1.6.
2. Shat.Br.,11.4.3.2.

3. Mahabharata 13.78.23.
4. Chhandegyopanishad,5.11.5.
5. Val. Ram., Lanka Kanda 114.65.
6. Ibid, Bala Kanda 29.3.
7. Mahabharata, Adi Parva 158.31.
8. Manusmiti, 9.232.
9. Gautama Dh. Sutra 6.21.22 and Apas. Dh. Sut. 2.5.11.59 and Mahabharata Vana Parva 133.1.
10. Uttara Ramachartira of Bhavabhuti 4.11.
11. *Ibid*, 4.10.
12. Shat. Br. 3.2.4,6.
13. Maitrayani Samhita.
14. Rigveda, 10.95.15.
15. Manusmiti, 9.14.15.
16. Mahabharata 11.73.17; Padma Purana, Stree Khanda 49.20.
17. Val. Ram., Ayodhya Kanda 12.100.
18. Varahamihira : Brihatsamhita 74.5.
19. *Ibid*, 74.
20. Bhavabhuti: Uttara Ramacarita.
21. Manusmiti, 2.214.
22. Lin U. Tang: Importance of Living.
23. Malavikagnimitra of Kalidasa., Act3.
24. V. S. Upadhyaya: Women in Rigveda.
25. Rigveda, 1.185.5.
26. *Ibid*, 6.75.5.
27. *Ibid*, 3.31.1.2.
28. Brichadarantopanished 6.4.17.
29. Manusmiti, 9.130.
30. Mahabharata Udyoga Parva 36-39.
31. Panchatantra 1.222.
32. Dr. A.S.Altekar: Position of Women in Hindu Civilization.
33. Dr. Rama Shankar Tripathi: Prachin Bharata ka Itihasa, p.40.
34. Panchatantra, 1.223.
35. Val. Ram., Balakanda, 67.23.

36. Mahabharata Adi Parva, 116.9.11.
37. *Ibid*, 157.37.
38. Shakuntala, 2.6.
39. Mahabharata Svargarohana Parva 5.

5

Motherhood, Child Rearing, *Samskaras* and Lifelong Guidance of the Mother

The *Rigveda* (5.47.6) says – 'Mothers weave clothes for their sons and teach the infants good deeds and thoughts.'

The man starts making use of his knowledge-senses right from the beginning. As an infant he imbibes knowledge within itself through these very senses – some elements thereof being based on intellect and others on experience, though experience itself is essentially a part of intellect. This knowledge, being born out of many perceptions and day-to-day occurrences, is the main factor in formation of *samskaras*. The bunch of *samskaras* brings about development of the child. The environment affects him substantially. His initial education is influenced by the combination of intellect, *samskaras* and environment and the educationists of today are constantly engaged in locating the elements governing the same and in inventing various systems of education.

In regard to education, Kautilya says that the son should be fondled only till the age of five. Thereafter, he should be kept under strict discipline for ten years, and when he enters the age of sixteen, we should behave with him like a friend. This shows that according to Kautilya sixth year is the right age for starting institutional education. But more accepted view is that of the *Smritikaras* who have laid down that ordinarily the *upanayana samskara* of a

Brahmana boy should be performed at the age of eight, that of a Kshatriya boy at eleven, and that of a Vaishya boy at twelve, whereafter he should be sent off to the *gurukula*. According to them, eighth year is ideal for start of Vedic studies and *brahmacharyashrama*. However, now start of basic education, both for boys and girls, at the age of five years has become the norm and modern educationists consider this the ideal age from psychological point of view.

In the context of basic education it must be remembered that no endeavour of the government or society could replace the infusion of *samskaras* by the mother. The mother imparts valuable training casually; she effortlessly teaches how to avoid pitfalls and how to extricate oneself from the same. The society or the government can never do so well enough. There are so many problems facing the nation that these seemingly small matters in day-to-day life are apt to be lost sight of. The environment has such a deep influence on the formation of the *samskaras* that this needs special attention right from childhood. The purity of environment and natural affection go to inculcate confidence, capability and a sense of security in the child. The *samskaras* acquired from the mother in the nascent form result in his physical, intellectual and moral development.

The child learns the mother tongue straight from the mother, and this is so for sons and daughters both. Both receive equal affection and attention from her. The father, while discharging his duties towards the child, tries to harmonize the internal and external circumstances with the domestic environment. But the training that a mother imparts most naturally can not be given even by the most resourceful nations. She starts discharging this duty while the child is still in the womb. The burden of its protection falls on her right from that stage.

Although modern thinkers have included child rearing in the syllabus for women's education, in actual practice no awareness has been created in the society as such. Many educated women display apathy towards motherhood and at times it assumes proportions of neglect. According to medical science, mother's milk is like nectar and has great medicinal properties and to deprive the child of the same is a crime. If the aim of education is merely to produce mechanical men, these early days could surely be neglected. But the man aims high, and therefore, childhood and its environment can not be neglected. As we have stated earlier, the greatest and the most effective contribution in creating a congenial atmosphere suitable for the child is that of the mother, and that is why she is said to be the first teacher. This goes to establish that child rearing should form a special feature of women's education, specially as the she-child is going to be a mother herself.

It is gradually dawning upon people that the atmosphere at home has an important role in education. The ancient educationists had carried out thorough research in this subject. The present educationists either do not think over the state before child-birth or they consider it unnecessary. But in a culture in which it is held that the creature enters the womb along with its accumulated *samskaras* of the previous lives, many primary religious rites are considered important. The initial *samskara* is *garbhadhana* whose purpose is to purify the egg and the semen that go to create life and to install a pure foundation in the womb. The *samskaras* acquired through the mother in the womb, and subsequently after birth, from the environment are permanent and much more valuable than academic education. This should be considered a part of over-all education and might be called *samskaric* education.

In this connection the utility of a maid should also be considered. There are many examples of good maids; and health, good conduct, desirable descent and dutifulness should be considered their attributes. Maids like, Panna are rare, who had saved Udai Singh, son of Sangrama Singh, from the cruel hands of Banabira by replacing him by her own son. Panna was from a decent Rajput family. Similarly, Kalidasa has referred to maids for Rama, Lakshmana etc.[1] He has described how the maid engaged for Raghu by Dilipa used to teach him good conduct so much so that Raghu had learnt to greet the elders with a bowed head at a very young age[2]. On the other hand, uneducated and uncultured maids or ayahs, who have become a necessity in many well-to-do families in society, can hardly be expected to impart any good qualities to the child. Feeling of affection in them for the child is unthinkable and to expect that they will create an awareness in it of the need to uphold family tradition, is futile.

In literature parental love (*vatsalya*) is classified as a form of *shringara rasa*. For the protection of the child *vatsalya* is essential. Along with allusions to mother's affection, there are references to filial love as well. In *Shakuntala* there is the story of Bharata, who was playing with the lion cubs in the *ashrama* of *maharshi* **Kashyapa**. Duskyanta, who had forgotten all about Shakuntala, could not resist picking him up in his lap, even though smeared with dust. Obviously, he had an unconscious awareness that Bharata was his son. The poet says in the words of Dushyanta, "I do not know why the playful child attracts me so. Blessed are they whose laps are dirtied by children, smeared with dust—children whose milk teeth are like buds and whose speech is still to evolve."[3]

We also learn of Arjuna reminiscing about Bhishma waiting on the bed of arrows for the sun to become Uttarayana when he says in the *Mahabharata*, "When I used to call him *tata* (father), he used to fondle me and say—I am not your *tata*, but *tata* of your *tata*." This is certainly a natural expression of ties of affection! Similarly, Mahakavi Bhavabhuti expresses the poignancy of mother's affection by imagining an incident in his *Uttara Ramacharita*[4] thus. Once Sita got separated from her sons, Lava and Kusha, in the jungle. At that time milk started oozing from her breasts as she remembered the occasion as their twelfth birthday. Along with affection, the mother feels the necessity of imparting teaching of great ideas and imbibing healthy *samskaras*. We may here quote Mahatma Gandhi, "I sincerely feel that the *samskaras* acquired during childhood run deep."[5] Further, "I can speak from experience that a child's education starts from the womb of his mother. The state of parents at the time of conception definitely affects the child. The child inherits the good or bad fruits of its mother's temperament and conduct during pregnancy. It starts copying the parents after birth. Since it is helpless, the responsibility for its development lies squarely on the parents."[6]

State of Development

There are numerous examples in Indian literature of the effect of the *samskaras* acquired during pregnancy on the later life. One such example appears in the *Uttara Ramacharita* of Bhavabhuti. Lakshmana got a mural painted in the bedroom of Lord Rama. Once when Rama and Sita were resting in that room, Lakshmana drew their attention to that mural. On seeing a scene therein Sita became curious and asked Lakshmana as to who were the two praying to Aryaputra (Rama). To this Lakshmana meekly replied, "*Devi*, these are *mantra*-blessed Jrimbhaka weapons. Krishashva had given these to sage Vishvamitra and the latter had given these to Aryaputra at the time of slaying of Taraka." Sita was pregnant at that time. It is said that the sight of this mural had such an indelible *samskara* on Lava and Kusha in the womb itself that they came to learn the use of these weapons right from birth. Later, when they had caught hold of Rama's horse of the *ashvamedha*, at the ensuing grave fight with the army of Ayodhya, Lava had made the entire army unconscious with this *astra*.[7]

The seeds of devotion were sown in Prahlada in his mother's womb. It is described in the *Shrimad Bhagavata* that Narada had sung praises of the Lord to Prahlada's mother during her pregnancy and that the foetus had imbibed the same meticulously.[8] Similarly, there is the story of *rishi* Aurva in the *Mahabharata*. Once many ***Kshatriyas*** decided to finish off the descendants of the sage Bhrigu. They destroyed all the males one by one, so much so that even the animals and birds could not help crying on hearing the wails of the women. One of the women was pregnant and these wails had a serious effect on the foetus. Now as soon as the child was born, he decided to destroy all the Kshatriyas. But the forefathers of the child, endowed with the great quality of forgiveness, managed to quench the fire of revenge in the child from their unseen abode. This child later came to be known as *rishi* Aurva.[9] *Maharshi Vasishtha* was a symbol of forgiveness and was endowed with great *brahmabala*. A strange incident of his life throws light on the influence of *samskara* on the foetus. The enemies had killed all the hundred sons of ***Vasishtha***. He was so overtaken by grief that he wanted to end his life. He jumped from mountain top, entered burning fire and threw himself in the speedy currents of the rivers Vyasa and ***Shutudru***. But the earth became too soft for him, the fire got quenched and the rivers started flowing very slowly. Finding that death was not in his hands, he returned to his *ashrama*. On the way he was astonished to hear chanting of Vedic *mantras* behind him and asked, "Who is chanting the *mantras* in a voice similar to that of my son, Shakti?"Adrishyanti, widow of his son, was following him. She replied, "O Great One, the sound is coming from the foetus of your son, Shakti, which I have been nursing for the last twelve years."[10] What happened was that when Shakti used to study Vedas, the pregnant Adrishyanti used to listen attentively and the foetus acquired the *samskara* of the chant. This goes to show that sounds do impinge upon the foetus and that forms *samskaras*. In the *Mahabharata*, we find a foetus speaking. Kuhoda, disciple of *maharshi* Uddalaka, was intelligent and devoted to his *guru*. So the *guru* was pleased and he taught him the *Vedas* in a short time and married his daughter to him. In due course when she was pregnant, a voice was heard coming from the womb. "Father! You study the *Vedas* whole night, but you do not appreciate the same fully"[11] Kuhoda used to practice and his wife used to listen carefully. This precocious child, later on, came to be known as Ashtavakra, whose creation *Ashtavakra Gita* is a gem in spirituality.

The story of Abhimanyu is only too well known. Once in the night Arjuna was narrating the art of formation of the *Chakravyuha* and the method of entering the same to the pregnant Subhadra, but he could not cover the method of getting out of it safely. The result was that Abhimanyu, who had learnt the art of breaking and entering the *Chakravyuha* in the womb itself, could not get out of it.[12]

The ancient specialists in embroyology knew only too well that the mother is instrumental in creating many types of indelible *samskaras* in the foetus. Keeping this in view, Vyasa in the conclusion of the *Mahabharata*, while enumerating the desirable benefits of listening to this epic, has specially laid down that pregnant women must listen to this narrative in order to give birth to a son or a lucky daughter.[13] In the story of Vidula it is stated that if a pregnant woman hears this, she will definitely give birth to a brave son.[14] All this is due to the fact that whatever a pregnant woman listens to carefully enters the foetus directly. So it is essential that during pregnancy both the *manas* and body of the mother and child are protected carefully. For this the environment must be healthy, pure and cultured. The woman should be afforded the facility of pure company and pure thoughts. Her room should have books, providing both healthy recreation and holy teachings; and pictures of saints, brave and selfless men. She should be beyond evil eyes and must shy away from pictures and books that are ugly and in bad taste. The *Garbhopanishad* describes how life enters the foetus in the seventh month, how it imbibes various attributes in the eighth month and how all sense organs get formed completely in the ninth month. At this stage the foetus gets to recollect all its deeds of previous lives – good or bad.[15] In the *Yajnavalkya Smriti* the sage has described at length how the *jiva* enters the womb and its gradual development. He avers that the basis of birth is not physical, but spiritual. In the union of the man and the woman when pure semen, ovum and blood mingle, Lord Himself receives the five primary elements; viz., earth, water, fire, sky (*akasha*) and air.[16]

This is also in keeping with the statement in the *Gita* that the living are part of the Almighty.[17] It says that in the cycle of birth, in the first month the five elements are in a thoroughly mixed up fluid condition. In the second month the foetus takes the shape of flesh. In the third month it acquires attributes of *akasha*; viz., minuteness, sound, hearing power etc.; those of *agni*; viz., sight, digestion, heat, fairness, light; those of *jala*; viz., coolness, juices, smoothness, hardness and softness; those of *prithivi*; viz., smell, essences, heaviness and image; and those of *vayu*; viz., touch, effort, harshness etc. The heart gets formed in this month. It is very essential to protect the foetus from this point onwards. It is also essential to fulfil the wishes of the mother, because by not doing so her heart suffers and that affects the heart of the foetus as well; so much so that the foetus could get deformed or could even die. The heart starts beating in the fourth month and the body parts formed earlier get stronger. Blood is formed in the fifth month, and complexion, nails and hair and power develop in the sixth. It acquires conscience and knowledge in the seventh month. *Vayu*, *pitta* and *kafa* – the three constituents of the body, according to Ayurveda, and nerves are formed at this stage. Skin, flesh and memory are formed in the eighth month. In this month a sort of internal energy agitates the foetus. Due to this a child born in the eighth month is never free from problems. In the ninth or the tenth month the *vayu* constituent predominates and the child gets born.

The author of the Nirukta opines that as soon as the baby comes in contact with the external atmosphere, it forgets previous births and *karmas*. Though it is generally true, cases of distinct memory of past life have come to light. Literature also mentions of great men and realized souls remembering incidents of their past lives. The Buddha remembered details of his past lives. Similarly Lord Krishna says, "You and I had many earlier births, which I know of, but you do not."[18] This also highlights that the Lord knew about past lives of Arjuna also. Such great men can certainly know of past lives of others. The *Mahabharata* narrates a dialogue between Yudhishthira and the Python, from which we learn that the Python remembered that he was King Nahusha in the previous life and that he had become a python due to the curse of *rishi* Agastya.[19] Similarly we know from *Shrimad Bhagavata* that King Nriga had to become a chameleon due to a curse and that he got liberated through the *darshana* of Shri Krishna. He remembered that he had to be born in this lowly manner due to some blunder on his part.[20] Those who believe in direct evidence only will not accept these stories. But from the accounts of *jatasmaras* even they will have to accept that the present life carries the *samskaras* of previous lives. Cases are known of families where nobody knew English or Sanskrit, yet the child could recite *Shlokas* of Sanskrit or talk fluently in English, though he had no occasion to hear any other language except his mother tongue. We hear of *jatasmaras*, who mentioned about their previous birth in some other town or village without any reference and whose narration of incidents etc. was found correct on verification.[21] It is scientfic knowledge that the defects in parents' sperm or ovum pass on to the child, causing congenital diseases; like leprosy, tuberculosis, asthma and V.D. etc. Nurturing /

refinement causes improvement in material objects, like plants or minerals. Similarly, *Shastric samskaras* could remove congenital defects. These *samskaras* certainly go towards creation of moral and spiritual force as well. In this connection the *Manusmriti* says, "The twice-born should perform *samskaras*, like *garbhadhana* etc., as envisaged in the *Vedas*. This leads to worldly and spiritual purity. The defects of the sperm/ovum and those related to pregnancy are removed by *samskaras* like, *garbhadhana, homa, jatakarma, chudakarma, upanayana* etc."[22]

Those who have assimilated the basic thought and *samskaras* of Indian culture along with gathering knowledge of Western civilization, do have faith in these *samskaras*. We have already talked of Mahatma Gandhi's statement that 'the child is certainly affected by the thoughts of his parents during his embryonic state'. Similarly, while commenting on the eleven *vratas*, like *brahmacharya* (celibacy), *aparigraha* (non-attachment) etc. propounded by Mahatma Gandhi, Dr. Rajendra Prasad, the late President of India, writes,"All the aspects of life, thoughts and attributes have been divided in three categories – *sattva, raja* and *tama*. Gandhiji's *vratas* are based on these. These are not at all new. Our *Shastras* have already enunciated the same. Their adherence is taught from the childhood, or we may say, from before birth itself, because rules have been laid down for discipline and control in begetting the child itself. The coming together of the man and the woman was not visualized as a shortlived pleasurable act only, but it was bound by certain rules considered necessary for preservation of the human race. Therefore, the child so born used to be cultured and well versed in rules of self-discipline and *samskaras*. Thus the *samskara* of the offspring started even before birth, at the time of co-habitation itself. There were many *samskaras* from birth till death, and even after death, which were meant to make the life full."[23]

The Mother, a Lifelong Guide

The motherhood has been eulogized in the statement of the *Mahabharata*.[24] It has also been counselled therein that the mother should be honoured like the father, *agni, guru* and *atman*, which can lead a man to conquer the earth and heavens.[25] *Manusmiti* has given the highest position to the mother on this account. In the *Manusmriti* the *guru* has been held to be ten times higher than the teacher, father a hundred times higher than the *guru*, and mother a thousand times higher than the father.[26] Similarly, in the *Taittiriya Upanishad* in the valedictory address given at the close of studies, the mother ranks highest amongst those who are to be held in high esteem.[27] The mother continues her efforts towards the well being of the child throughout her life. That includes its care, prayer for its good and steadfastness on the right path. Just as the culmination of womanhood lies in motherhood, the aim of motherhood is centred round upbringing of the child. The child derives right inspiration, love and goodwill from the mother, Therefore, to accord a honourable place for the mother in society is to honour the women as a class. That is why the *Upanishads* have enjoined upon the student, when returning home after completion of studies, not only to be alert in discharging his duties towards *dharma, swadhyaya* (self study), *Vedas*, gods and ancestors, but also to be truthful and devoted towards the mother and father throughout his life.[28]

There is an incident in the *Chhandogya Upanishad* as to how a mother can make her child truthful. In those days a student, at the time of entry in *brahmacharya ashrama*, had to mention his *gotra*. A boy, known as Satyakama Jabala, wanted to enter *brahmacarya ashrama*. When he asked his mother, Jabala, about his *gotra*, she said," Son, I do not know what your *gotra* is. I used to do multifarious chores at places when you were born. So I can not say who your father is and what your *gotra* is. My name is Jabala and your name is Satyakama. You call yourself Satyakama

Jabala."[29] Had Jabala wanted to hide her conduct, she could have given out some imaginary *gotra*. But she did not want an untruth to mar the character of her son, and gave him the *mantra* of truthfulness and righteousness. Satyakama went to the *ashrama* of Haridrumata of Gautama *gotra*, requested him for entry and repeated verbatim what his mother had told about his *gotra*. The *guru*, impressed by his truthfulness, treated him a Brahmana and took him in as his disciple. There is a lot of controversy regarding whether Satyakama Jabala was a Brahmana or Shudra. Shankaracharya in his *Bhashya* of *Chhandogyopanishad* (6.4.2) has given resons for treating Satyakama a Brahmana. He holds that Jabala, being engrossed in the service of the guests, could not find time to aseertain the *gotra* of her husband and he suddenly died. He agrees that Haridrumata would have accepted Satyakama to be a Brahmana, as a non-Brahmana was unlikely to be so truthful. A reference is invited to the author's book, *Upanishad Rahasya* Part I, Chapter 2—*Upanishadon ki Sarvabhaumikata* for a conclusive explanation. Be what it may, there is no denying the fact that the teacher valued truthfulness the most as an adjunct to entry in the '*grihasthashrama*' and that the credit for teaching truthfulness at all cost to the son goes to Jabala. The story of Suniti, mother of Dhruva, who showed him the path of devotion to God, runs in the *Bhagavata* thus. King Uttanapada had two queens, Suniti and Suruchi. He was totally under the spell of Suruchi. One day, seeing that the King was fondling Uttama, the son of Suruhi, Dhruva, too, got on the lap of the father. On this, the King at the behest of Suruhi, rebuked Dhruva and the step-mother told him that the honour was reserved for her own child, and that, if he so desired, the only course open for him was to perform *tapas* and please God to get born as her son. Though Dhruva was only five years old, he took the rebuff to heart.

Sumati was exceptionally devoted to God. Though the co-wife had spoken about obtaining the boon from God in sarcasm, Sumati who knew the power of *tapas*, exhorted Dhruva to imbibe real devotion to God. Moved by intense feeling of renunciation and *bhakti*, she consoling Dhruva, told him that Suniti was correct and said, "The King is even ashamed of calling me his wife. But if you want to sit on the lap of your father, there is nothing wrong in it. There is nothing that can not be achieved by devotion to God. Even Brahma has earned the title of *Parameshthi* through His favour. The example of your grandfather, Manu, is right before you, who had earned divinity by performing *yajnas* devotedly through grace of God. So seek the protection of the Almighty with unflinching devotion." Following the advice of his mother, Dhruva performed such severe *tapas* that God was pleased with him and, in due course, Uttanapada made him his successor.[30]

In literature we come across many instances of lifelong guidance given by mothers and achieving of all round success through their inspiration. Some of these are given below.

It has been ingrained in our social ethos that it is a holy deed to listen to the story of Vidula. She was not only a guide to her son, but has left an eternal example to be emulated by Indian women as a whole. Even Kunti was deeply influenced by her character. Kunti herself occupies a unique position as a mother. Her husband, Pandu, died when her children were infants, even the co-wife had followed her husband and the burden of bringing up the infants fell on her squarely. Kunti stood like an epitome of courage. Even though all facilities were made available for proper upbringing of the Pandavas, they were not secure. Thus far Duryodhana had been considering himself the sole successor to the Hastinapura throne, but his hopes were shattered with arrival of the real successor, Yudhishthira. It became the aim of Duryodhana to do away with this obstacle and that of Kunti to be vigilant in ensuring security of her sons. She had realized that the mild Yudhishthira had exceptional intelligence and serenity. So she cautioned him to be constantly vigilant and continued to guide him to avoid dangers. After burning down of Lakshagriha, when she was staying with her children in Ekachakra, she considered it her duty to protect the Brahmana family that had given them shelter from the demon Baka. She pressed Bhima to kill the demon and thus saved not only the Brahmana family, but the entire town, teaching thereby how to return gratitude.

Kunti feared that Yudhishthira, out of his inherent kindness, might give up the duty of a Kshatriya to avoid terrible outcome of a war and take to *sanyasa*. Thus when Lord Krishna had failed in his mission in Hastinapura and had got a blank reply from Duryodhana that he would not give up land as miniscule as the point of a needle, Kunti had sent the well known message through him for Yudhishthira, following the example of Vidula, not to forget Kshatra *dharma*.

Ordinary humans lose courage in adversity. But great men are able to change the course of Time. The teachings of mothers; like Vidula, Kunti, and Jijabai have been instrumental in framing the character of such men. The story of Vidula is akin to teachings in the Gita in regard to highlighting *svadharma*. The ruler of Sindhu, had suddenly attacked and conquered the kingdom of Sanjaya, son of Vidula. Sanjaya was a mere boy and had run away from the battlefield and hidden himself. Vidula exhorted him to follow Kshatra *dharma*, even if it meant getting killed in the battle. This aroused his latent sense of duty. Vidula cared in the least for motherly affection, and made Sanjaya give up bodily attachment and realize the immortality of soul. Sanjaya fought and ultimately became victorious. Vidula's immortal words are valid to this day towards exhortation to the nation.[31]

Two incidents in the *Mahabharata* would rank Kunti amongst the greatest women. One is the message referred to above enjoining upon Yudhishthira to follow Kshatra *dharma* rigidly. She had advised Yudhishthira to give up hopes of regaining his rights through peaceful means and not waste time in waiting for a suitable opportunity. She had propounded that a king or a valiant person is not slave to circumstances, he creates the same.[32] Her words—'the time for which Kshatriyas are born, has come'—[33] would go to inspire one and all to be ready to sacrifice their lives in fulfilment of duty. The purpose behind this exhortation was not procurement of worldly pleasures, but for fighting injustice, because she held that it was the primary duty of the Pandavas to secure their part of the kingdom from the Kauravas through *dharmayuddha*. The second was fifteen years after the *Mahabharata* war when Vidura, Gandhari, Dhritarasthra and Kunti had set about to leave for *vanaprastha*. The Pandavas, specially Yudhishthira, made repeated entreaties with Kunti to stay back, but she declined. On this Yudhisthira taunted her as to why she had encouraged them to go to war, if that is what she was going to do. Kunti still did not relent and reminded him that she had exhorted them to fight only for their rights. Finally, while taking leave of her sons, she preached to them, "Be steadfast in *dharma*, and keep your thinking high." Any nation will be proud of mothers with such lofty ideals.

Madalasa, Queen of Ritudhvaja, was an accomplished *yogi*. All her four sons, whom she had taught herself, followed the spiritual path. Similarly, Sumitra will be ever remembered for guiding Lakshmana on the right path. When Lakshmana goes to his mother to seek her permission to go with Rama and Sita to the forests, she does not ask him to rule over Ayodhya with Bharata. She encourages him in his determination by saying, "You are lucky that you are a worshipper of Rama. You are born for *vanavasa*. Son, do not ever fail in your duty towards him. This is the path for you, whether you are happy or otherwise. Good men are required to follow their elder brothers. The *dharma* of our Ikshvaku clan is to perform sacrifices, to give alms and to end the life in battlefield. You should consider Rama to be your father, Sita to be your mother and the forests your Ayodhya. Go happily."[34] Goswami Tulasidasa, too, has expressed somewhat similar feelings through Sumitra in the *Ramacharita Manasa*.[35]

Gandhari is immortal in the history of culture on account of her character, far sightedness and sense of justice. She had repeatedly advised Duryodhana to give up injustice and follow the path of righteousness. She warned him not to overestimate his might. She believed that Krishna was an incarnation of God and that the Pandavas would be able to defeat the Kauravas as they had the protection of Krishna. When the emissary of Dhritarashtra, Sanjaya, on return from Upaplavya, was narrating the pithy reply of Yudhishthira before the royal court, Duryodhana had committed insult of the court by leaving in a huff. Similarly, when Krishna was making his historic effort for a treaty at the specially called court, Duryodhana had again exhibited his callous nature. On these occasions even though great personages like, Bhishma, Vidura and Dronacharya were present, Duryodhana did not listen to them and Dhritarashtra was forced to send for Gandhari to make him see reason. In the entire family only Gandhari had some influence over him. She advised him to follow the path of justice and control his ill manners. On the first and all other days of the *Mahabharata* war Duryodhana sought the blessings of his mother for victory. But like a brave mother she only exhorted him to fight bravely and never once blessed him to be victorious, as she strongly felt that his was not a just cause. She would only repeat 'Victory lies where *dharma* is.'

The old tradition has continued. The contribution of Jijabai in character formation of Shivaji was no less than that of Samartha Guru Ramadasa. It was from her that the first inspiration to save the Hindu religion was received by

Shivaji. Similarly, the Rajput history is full of anecdotes of mothers who had exhorted their sons at critical times to tread the path of duty. In this connection the mother of the ruler of Amalanera under Chittor is remembered with great respect. The story of the maid, Panna, who had sacrificed her son to save the six year old son of Rana Sanga, Udaya Simha, from the sword of Banavira, is well known. When, trying to seek refuge for the child, she approached the ruler of Amalanera, he was scared. At that juncture his mother reprimanded him severely saying, in the words of James Todd, in his '*History of Rajasthan*' – "Loyalty is never deterred by fear or difficulties. This child is your master, son of Sanga. Fear not, with God's grace things will turn out to be helpful."

In conclusion, we must remember the mother of Mohandas Karamchand Gandhi, who was thoroughly brought up in Indian culture. Follower of a strict moral code, she had a great hand in forming the character of Gandhiji. In the adverse environment of those days, when Gandhiji was leaving for England at the age of nineteen in 1888, his devout mother had obtained three vows from him; viz. not to eat meat or fish, not to drink and not to womanize. In spite of distractions, Gandhiji had kept up these vows.

References

1. Raghuvamsha of Kalidasa, 10.78.
2. Raghuvamsha of Kalidasa, 3.25.
3. Shakuntala, 7.17.
4. Uttara Ramacharita, 3.17.
5. Mahatma Gandhi: Autobiography 7th. ed. p. 39.
6. *Ibid*, p. 235.
7. Uttara Ramacharita.
8. Shrimadbhagavata., 7.7.
9. Mahabharata, Adi Parva, ch. 178-179.
10. Mahabharata, Adi Parva, ch. 177.12.15.

11. Mahabharata, Vana Parva, 132.10.
12. For greater detail refer to Dharmaraja Yudhishthira, III ed. 1967: Chandra Bali Tripathi.
13. Mahabharata, Svargarohana Parva 5.52.
14. Ibid, V. Parva, 1.36.19.
15. Garbhopanishad.
16. Yajngavalkya Smriti.
17. Gita, 15.7.
18. Gita, 4.5.
19. Mahabharata, Vana Parva: Ajagar-Yudhisthira dialogue.
20. Shrimadbhagavata., Sk. 10th, Adh. 64.
21. Researches regarding rebirth are being carried out in the West. Dr. Stevenson of Virginia University, U.S.A., Chairman, Deptt. of Psychology and Neurology is out on tour in India to learn about the *jatasmaras*. He has contacted father of Prakash Chandra Varshney of Chatanagara, Mathura to know about the incidents of the past life, which the latter remembers. (This pertains to the seventies when the original book was written).
22. Manusmiti, 26-27.
23. Rajendra Prasad: Bapu ke Qadamon men p.219.
24. Mahabharata, Shanti Parva 342.18.
25. *Ibid*, Vana Parva 159.14.
26. Manusmiti., 2.145.
27. Tatt. Up. Shksa Valli 11.2.
28. *Ibid* .
29. Chhandogya Up. 6.4.2.
30. Shrimadbhagavata., 4.7.
31. Mahabharata, Udyoga Parva 135.29.30.
32. *Ibid*, 137.10.
33. *Ibid*, 132.16.
34. Val. Ram, Ayodhya Kanda 402.6, 7, 10.
35. Rama Charita Manasa, Ayodhya Kanda.

6

The Basis of Social Evolution: *Varna, Ashrama* and Education

Varna, Ashrama

Indian culture has certain fundamental strengths that have prevented dismemberment of its society. The most important elements in any social structure are related to conduct, and India has always been alive to this. On the other hand, the Western society has failed to realize this basic fact, resulting in laxity in conduct, including unrestricted sexual behavior, and undue stress on acquisition of wealth. Indian society was divided in four *varnas* according to capabilities (not colours as wrongly defined by some Western scholars). Similarly, the four *ashramas* denoted four stages of life. Education and *samskaras* have developed on those lines right from the Vedic times in India.

In the Indian tradition the social structure is believed to have emanated from the Divine Being (Purusha) at the beginning of creation. The *Rigveda* in a *mantra*[1] states that from the mouth of that Being were born Brahmanas, from arms, Kshatriyas; from thighs, Vaishyas and from legs, Shudras. The entire Vedic literature confirms this concept. The *Manusmrti*[2] and *Mahabharata* repeat the same and Lord Krishna calls it eternal. He declares that He created the four *varnas* according to classification of *gunas* and *karmas*.[3]

It is to be appreciated that the interdependence of the *varnas* is similar to that of body parts. Peace and happiness in society are possible only with harmony amongst these four *varnas*, like harmonious functioning of body parts for proper development of the body and soul. Just as it is ridiculous to assign higher and lower values to various body parts, there is no place in Vedic thought for feeling of high and low amongst the *varnas*. The contrary trends in later literature or social behaviour are certainly not in keeping with the original principle. The *Bhagavadgita*, while expounding the basis of *varnashrama*, states that the very structure of the world is based on the three *gunas*—*sattva*, *rajas* and *tamas* and unequal development of these *gunas* among individuals gives rise to difference in their capabilities. The activities in any developed society are, broadly speaking, divided into areas of knowledge, power, wealth and labour. Thus if the society is classified according to *gunas*, the four divisions or *varnas* as above are certainly logical.

In the system of *varna dharma* a person of a particular Varna performs his allotted duties conscientiously without interfering with those of another *varna*. He dedicates his efforts to God and thus ensuring stability of society, realizes progress in the world and his ultimate aim.[4] The famous Greek philosopher, Plato, had visualized a similar society in his priceless work, '*Republic*', but no efforts were made in Greece to give it a practical shape. Thus the *varna dharma* is, no doubt, a unique heritage for India!

Education

With the establishment of *varnas* in Vedic society, rules were framed in respect of education as well. It appears **Shudras**, though entitled to education, were not considered fit for study of the *Vedas*, and on this account, for *brahmacharyashrama*. As per *Manusmrti* and other *Smritis* these were confined to the twice-born (*dvijati*). Adherence to *brahmacharya* and study of the *Vedas* being considered the essential aspects, the system was called *brahmacharya* system.

Being imparted in *gurukulas,* it was also called *gurukula* system. In olden days, large *Ashramas* of *rishis* were located in forests close to the cities or villages. These were centres of not only spirituality, but were meant to impart teaching in various subjects as in universities. The *guru* or the *acharya* was generally a *grihastha* (householder) and the *brahmachari* was like a family member and devoted to the *guru* and his wife, thus enjoying a sort of parental love in the process. Some *ashramas* had many *acharyas* and *upadhyayas* and could house as many as even ten thousand students. The head of such *ashramas* was called *kulapati. Maharshi* Kanva, in whose *ashrama* Shakuntala was born and brought up, was a famous *kulapati. Maharshi* Kashyapa, in whose *ashrama* Bharata, the son of Dushyanta and originator of Bharata clan, was brought up, was his contemporary. We hear of famous *rishis,* like Vishwamitra, Vasishtha,Valmiki and Agastya etc. in the *Ramayana* age, in whose *gurukulas* arts and science were taught. In the *Mahabharata* age famous *ashramas* were those of Vedavyasa, Bharadvaja, Shaunaka etc. It is in the *ashrama* of Shaunaka in the Naimisharanya, where thousands of *rishis* lived and where this famous *kulapati* had performed a *yajna* lasting twelve years at which *rishi* Ugrashrava had narrated the *Mahabharata.* At Haridwar was located the *gurukula* of Bharadwaja, where along with the teaching of *Vedas,* military sciences were also taught. *Rishi* Agnivesha, after acquiring mastery in archery from *Maharshi* Bharadwaja, had imparted this knowledge to Dronacharya and Drupada at this *gurukula.* Similarly Sudama and Krishna were taught the *Vedas* at the *ashrama* of rishi Sandipani in Avanti. At these *ashramas* numerous *rishis* used to contemplate on Brahma and teach Brahmavidya to deserving students, which led to creation of *Aranyakas* and *Upanishads.* In the same tradition Vyasa after compiling the four Vedas in his *ashrama*, had enjoined upon his principal disciples, Vaishampayana, Jaimini, Sumantu and Paila etc. to propagate the *Vedas*.

In the *Mahabharata* age we also find large *vidyapithas* in large cities, like Hastinapura. Kauravas and Pandavas had obtained their initial training at the institution of *acharya* Kripa at Hastinapura. It was here that Dronacharya had established a large institution for specialized training in military sciences for them.

Ancient Universities at Takshashila, Nalanda, Vikramashila and Vallabhi

We have no evidene of a large university in the *Ramayana* and earlier times, though kings of the Raghu clan were great patrons of learning.[5] Takshashila university was, however, well established in *Mahabharata* age, Dhaumya being mentioned as its *acharya*. Most probably it was established by the ruler of that area, Taksha, son of Bharata. It is here that later on Janmejaya performed the Naga *yajna* (serpent sacrifice), at which Vaishampayana had narrated the *Mahabharata* for the first time collectively.

The fame of Takshashila had spread throughout India in the 7th Cen. B.C. and students used to go there from far and wide to learn various arts and sciences. Even students from renowned centres of learning; like, Kashi, Ujjaini, and Mithila used to go there for specialized learning in specific subjects. Prasenajita, the heir apparent of Koshala and a contemporary of the Buddha, was educated there. The world famous grammarian, Panini, Kautilya, author of *Arthashastra*, and Jivaka, the great master of Ayurveda, were all educated here. It is also seen from the Greek accounts that at the time of Alexander's invasion Takshashila was a great educational centre, especially for Indian philosophy. Later, the repeated onslaughts of the barbarian Hunas destroyed it completely so much so that Fa-hien, the Chinese traveller in the 5th Cen. A.D. found nothing worth mentioning.

This great loss was to some extent made good with the establishment of Nalanda university in the 5th Cen. This place was sacred in the Buddhist world being the place of birth and death of a principal disciple of Buddha, Sariputra. It soon became an international centre of research in Buddhist religion and philosophy. The Gupta kings, though mostly followers of *Sanatana Dharma,* were very tolerant and they liberally contributed towards development of the university. Though in the Golden Age of the Guptas all parts of the empire witnessed a unique spurt in fine arts, sciences, literature etc., it was especially noticeable at Nalanda. Dr. Agarwal quotes Yuan Chuang as having seen a 80 ft. copper statue of Buddha erected by King Purna Varma, among many other huge statues, at Nalanda in the 7th cen.A.D.[6]

The excavations carried out at Nalanda reveal that the institution had seven or eight huge halls and three hundred class rooms. The huge Buddha statue at the entrance was a constant reminder to the students to follow the *dharma* steadfastly. The buildings were multi-storeyed, about which the poet says, "their tops were touching the clouds and these were so beautiful as if Brahma had created these Himself."[7] The *viharas* (monasteries) were located separately. Later, when Itsing visited Nalanda in the 7th cen., he found that the number of *viharas* had gone up to seven hundred. Many students from China, Korea and Tibet etc. studied at this university. The university had a huge library, accommodated in big buildings called 'Ratnasagara' and 'Ratnodadhi'. The entire complex was known as 'Dharmagarbha'. Its main auditorium could house eight thousand persons. In addition, there were six *vidyapithas* with four senior *acharyas* for each. Education, including boarding and lodging, was free for students. Nalanda was destroyed by the fanatic, Bakhtiar Khalji in the 12th. century A.D. The monks were put to the sword and even the priceless library was burnt down. Many arts and sciences were lost for ever.

When Nalanda was at the zenith of its fame, King Dharmapala of Bengal established Vikramashila university in the 8th century The same Bakhtiar Khalji destroyed this as well, including the *viharas* and the huge library, and massacred thousands of *bhikshus*. Among other famous universities were the one at Udantapuri in Orissa, and Vallabhi in Saurashtra. The latter, which had flourished from the 5th century till 12th century suffered a set back in 727AD. due to invasion of the Arabs, but it soon recovered. No university was established during the Muslim rule.

In the Upanishadic age Mithila vied with Kashi as a great centre of learning as evidenced from a statement of Ajatashatru, king of Kashi, to Dripta Balaki in *Brihadaranyaka Upanishad*.[8] Likewise, Panchala was also famous for learning. That there was high degree of literacy, and in certain areas, complete, is borne by the proud declaration of Ashwapati, king of Kekaya, "In my kingdom there is no thief, no miser, no drunkard, no non-worshipper of family fire, no illiterate, no depraved man or woman."[9] In times to come, though huge *gurukulas* and universities no longer survived, Kashi and Mithila kept the torch of learning burning and the *vidyapithas* at Ayodhya, Nadia, Pataliputra, Kanchi, Dhara, Ujjain, Malakheda, Tanjore and Kalyani etc. continued under the patronage of selfless people without state assistance. In all parts of the country, specially in the South, the *pathashalas* attached to temples and *mathas* continued to impart education and there was no dearth of teachers who would work gratis. People donated generously towards this noble cause.

Study of *Vedas* and Rules of *Brahmacharyashrama*

Teaching of *Vedas* was the primary duty of the Brahmanas and the teachers at the *gurukulas* were all Brahmanas, who accepted no remuneration. Every student, whether son of a poor Brahmana or a king, had to bring alms from the near by villages and hand over to the *guru* and all expenses were met due to simple living. Without exception he had to bring fuel from the forest, removing all feelings of disparity and thus inculcating spirit of self help.

There was a special provision to perform *yajnopavita* of a Brahmana boy desirous of erudition in the fifth year, that of a Kshatriya boy keen to imbibe valour, in the sixth year and that of a Vaishya boy with a talent for trading, in the eighth year and then to send to the *gurukula*.[10] The customary age of entry in *brahmacharyashrama* was the eighth, eleventh and twelfth year for a Brahmana, Kshatriya and Vaishya boy respectively.[11] No clear basis for this distinction is available. However, in regard to Brahmanas, it was probably felt the boy needed more time for acquiring knowledge of his '*swadharma*', comprising of *sama, dama, tapa* etc.[12] Rigid adherence to celibacy was a must in *brahmacharyashrama*. The *Shruti* has laid down that—"the gods were able to conquer death through *tapas* and *brahmacharya*."[13] The *Gita* says—"Observance of *brahmacharya* , is for realization of Brahma."[14] The period of Vedic study at the *ashrama* was twelve years as would appear from the teaching of Uddalaka Aruna to his son, Shvetaketu, in the *Chhandogya Upanishad*.[15] *Manusmiti* had ruled that the *Vedas* should be studied for thirty six or eighteen years at the *gurukula*, but in practice there was no hard and fast rule in regard to a specific period.[16] Here it may be mentioned, in passing, that although there is no specific mention of *brahmacharyashrama* in the *Vedas* or *Brahmanas*, it does not mean that the system did not exist at that time, because the *Rigveda* and *Atharvaveda* do mention the term '*brahmachari*' and so do the *Taittiriya Samhita* and the *Shatapatha Brahmana*, the term *brahmacharya*. At the *gurukula* the teacher paid individual attention to the students and the student was free to complete the Vedic studies in more or less time depending on his mental capability.

Women and Vedic Studies

The *Bhagavata* mentions that "Vyasa found that some Brahmanas, who were so only in name, and women and Shudras were not getting the benefit of Vedic *mantras,* and so he created the *Mahabharata* for their good."[17] But this in itself does not prove that women were never eligible for *brahmacharyashrama* or Vedic studies. Rather, it is a matter of pride that in our culture women in the Vedic age not only studied the *Vedas,* but some of them were so gifted as to create *mantras* and become *mantradrashtas,* like *rishis.* Vak, the daughter of *rishi,* Ambhrina, was the *rishika* of the famous *Devisukta* of the *Rigveda.* Similarly Ghosha, Apala, Lopamudra, Vishwavara, Sikata, Surya, Indrani, Sarparajnin, Mamata, Yami, Romasha, Juhu, Nivavari, Urvashi, Shraddha etc. were *rishikas* which underlines the importance of women in our culture. In Vedic times *brahmacharya* for women was lauded as seen from the *mantra* in the *Atharva Veda*—"*brahmacharya* is at the root of a king's ability to protect the nation, *acharya*'s ability to teach the students and a virgin's success in finding an able young husband."[18]

Upanayana and study of Vedas for women have been accepted by Harita *Dharmashastra* as well. It divides women in groups—those desirous of being *brahmacharinis* could go in for ***upanayana*** and Agnihoma, study *Vedas* and take to living by alms; and those wanting to marry early could get ***upanayana*** only and acquire Brahmavidya.[19] *Yama Smriti* confirms that women were entitled to Vedic studies and *brahmacharya.* It, however, lays down that they could study *Vedas* from father, brother or uncle at home itself.

The antiquity of *Grihyasutras,* created before *Smritis* and after Vedic *Samhitas* and *Brahmanas,* is accepted by scholars. The Gohila and Ashvalayana *Grihyasutras* have mentioned *brahmacharyashrama* and ***upanayana*** for women. In the Gohila *Grihyasutra* it has been stated that at marriage the groom, leading the bride, wearing *yajnopavita* before the sacred fire, chants a specific Rigvedic *mantra*.[20] Similarly in the Ashvalayana *Grihyasutra* it has been stated in the context of *samavartana samskara* performed at the end of Vedic studies that 'The Brahmana *brahmachari*, after smearing both his hands with sacred paste, should first smear his face, the Kshatriya one, both his arms, the Vaishya one, his stomach and the *brahmacharini*, her private parts.'[21] When we look at the statements in other sacred and temporal literature, we do conclude that women were not deprived of Vedic studies in that age. In the *Ramayana* age we find Valmiki mentioning that in order to invoke heavenly blessings for successful conclusion of the function appointing Rama as heir apparent, '***Kaushalya***, putting on *Kausheya* clothes, performed the holy rites, including chanting of *mantras* and *havana*.'[22] Valmikiya *Ramayana*, in the description of the exile days, describes how particular Sita was about *sandhya*, like Rama.[23] The reason that Rama gave for his hope to find Sita on the banks of the river, after she had been carried away by Ravana was – 'knowing that it is dusk time Sita will definitely come to the river bank for *sandhya*.'[24] It hardly needs mention that chanting of Vedic *mantras* is an essential part of *sandhya*.

Kalidasa, too, has mentioned about Vedic studies and Agnihotra by women. He writes in Kumarasambhava- 'When Parvati after bath, wearing tree bark attire, was chanting Veda *mantras* during *havana*, even the *rishis* greeted her, because age is no criterion in recognition of spiritual attainment'.[25]

The Situation in the Upanishadic Period

It can not be said for certain that Vedic studies and observance of *brahmacharya* were prerequisites for ***Brahmavidya***. However, *Mundakopanishad* does lay down in a mantra—'Only those who are conversant with the Vedas, are observing their tenets, and are performing *havana* in the sacred fire, known as Ekarshi, and have performed Shirovrata as prescribed, are entitled to learn Brahmavidya.'[26]

Among women, the name of Maitreyi has been immortalized in the history of spiritual learning by the *Brahadaranyaka Upanishad*. It describes how the self-realized *rishi*, Yajnavalkya, had made an offer to his wives, Katyayani and Maitreyi—"I want to divide my possessions between the two of you to take to *sanyasa*." Maitreyi had rejected the offer and proclaimed the immortal words, 'What shall I do with that which can not make me free from the cycle of births? Please impart your knowledge to me.'[27] The *rishi* taught Brahmavidya to her[28] and ranked her amongst the great *brahmajnanis*.

Gargi Vachaknavi was a *brahmavadini*, who had impressed even Yajnavalkya. In those days Mithila used to be a centre of learning and under the patronage of Janaka, big conferences used to be held there and philosophers used to assemble from far and wide to discuss Brahmavidya. At one such conference, when everybody had accepted defeat due to the erudition of Yajnavalkya, Gargi flooded him with serious questions, so much so that the *rishi* had to put a stop to the discussions by saying—'Your questions belong to the realm of mystery and such questions are not meant to be raised and answered in public.'[29] We hear of a similar conference held in Panchala (Brh, Up., 6.2.1). Ajatashtru, king of Kashi, had explained secrets of Brahmavidya to Dripta Balaki. While answering questions of Dripta Balaki, Ajatashtru remonstrated that it was not in order that a Brahmana should pray to a Kshatriya to impart Brahmajnana to him. (Brh, Up., 2.1.14) The *Chhandogya* Upanishad (5.11.5) mentions Ashvapati, king of Kekaya, elaborating secrets of 'Vaishwanara Vidya to *brahmavettas*;

like, Aupamanyava, Satyayajnan, Indradyumna. There is ample evidence that in those days Brahmavidya was not limited only to Brahmanas.

The tradition of Vedantic knowledge amongst women continued throughout the Vedic period. *Uttara Ramacharita* mentions the story of a woman, named Attreyi, who, on being questioned by sage Agastya as to why she had left the *ashrama* of sage Valmiki and come to her for study of Brahmavidya, had replied – 'Firstly, I could not match Lava and Kusha in studies and secondly, the *kulapati*, being busy in writing the *Ramayana* was unable to pay proper attention to teaching.'[30] This illustrates the keenness of women to learn Brahmavidya in those days.

The Roots of Co-education in *Samavartana Samskara*

The women were allowed to study alongside men without purdah in those days, an example being that of Attreyi above. The process of *Samavartana Samskara* described in Ashvalayana *Grihyasutra* supports the practice of co-education in the *gurukulas* at the beginning of the *brahmacharya* system. Somehow co-education came to an end in the later Vedic age and women were taught Vedas at home.

With the passage of time, recitation of *Vedas* and process of *yajnas* became more and more complex and decline in mental faculties caused a serious problem. It came to be realized that a minor mistake in the chanting of *mantras* could cause more harm than good, an example of which has been given by Panini.[31] He says," *A mantra* that is devoid of the correct sound or letter or that which has been wrongly employed, does not lead to the desired purpose. Becoming a *vajra* in the shape of a word, it kills the chanter himself, just as Vritrasura was killed due to a faulty chant."[32] Such beliefs created a fear in the society and not only Vedic studies suffered, but women came to be kept out of the same.

We find that in the detailed rules of *brahmacharya* in the *Manusmriti*, there is no mention of women's right to ***upanayana*** or Vedic studies. Rather, these were considered unnecessary for them. At the time when *Manusmriti*[33] was given the present form, it was propounded that marriage itself was Vedic *samskara* for a woman, caring for the husband was *gurukula* and managing the household was the worship of the sacred Fire for her. With the relaxation in the provision of *brahmacharya* for the women, the age of marriage started coming down. Decline in her intellect ensued and she started losing her independence.

In the heyday of Vedic civilization women were not only free to study *Vedas*, but they participated in political institutions; like '*sabhas*' and '*Samitis*' and religious conferences, like '*vidathas*' at the time of *yajnas*. In the Rigvedic *mantra* for marriage the groom says to the bride—"you will be honoured to speak at the *vidatha*".[34] In due course when women stopped going to the *gurukulas*, their participation at the conferences also came to a stop. *Maitrayani Samhita* indicates this when it says—'That is why only men go to the *sabhas*, and not women.'[35] It appears that this had come in force before the time of King Dasharatha, because Valmiki mentions that only men of all *varnas* were called at the *sabha* for considering the proposal to crown Rama as heir apparent. Open participation of women at *sabhas* had definitely ended by the *Mahabharata* time. The words of Draupadi corroborate this view. When Dushshasana was dragging her to the court after Yudhishthira had lost her at the dice game, she reproachfully remarked, "I have heard that in the past they never took a woman following the path of *dharma* to the *sabha*. That ancient *Sanatana dharma* seems to have disappeared for the Kauravas."[36]

Profile of Women's Education

There was adequate arrangement of education for women in the higher rungs of society and experienced and scholarly old men were deputed for the purpose. We see that at her *swayamvara,* Damayanti due to her advanced education, was able to see through the deceit of Indra, Varuna,Yama and Agni, who had appeared as Nala, as she had learnt the ways of identifying gods.[37] She had learnt from the aged that 'nobody dies before his time'.[38] We also find that Kunti, while giving her message to Krishna on return from his failed mission at Hastinapura, had stated, 'Listen to one more example which I have learnt from the old'.[39] Draupadi, too, confirms that she had 'heard the *varna dharma* from the Brahmanas regarding wife being protector of the husband by virtue of her protecting his child in her womb.'[40] She further says, "Success and failure are transient. So thinking, I am waiting for better days for my husbands..."[41] This exhibition of patience and utilization of acquired knowledge on her part point to her liberal education.

Cottage industry used to be taught to women in Vedic times, and the process continued. House management and domestic accounting formed an essential part of women's education. Inclusion of dance, music and painting in their education continues to this day.

Syllabus and Field of Education

The statement in the *Manusmriti* that "the *brahmacharin* should study the three Vedas in the *gurukula* for 36, 18, 9 years or till he can complete"[42] does not describe the syllabus fully. According to *Shatapatha Brahmana, anushasana* was an essential part of Vedic studies[43], which has been explained by the commentator, Sayana, as including Education, Kalpa, Grammar, Nirukta, Chhanda and Astronomy. Teaching of many other branches was added during the Upanishadic period. It is seen from the

Chhandogya Upanishad that the sage Narada was questioned by the Sanatkumaras, before they would teach him Brahmavidya as per his request regarding what arts and sciences he had learnt. The sage had replied, 'I have read the four *Vedas*, History, *Puranas*, *Pitri Vidya* (science of ancestors), Astrology, Daiva Vidya (Natural science), *Nidhividya* (science of wealth), *Vakovakya* (elocution), *Ekayana*, *Deva Vidya* (God science), *Brahma Vidya*, *Bhuta Vidya* (ghost science), Kshatra *Vidya* (military science), Astronomy, *Sarpa Vidya* (serpent science), *Devajnana Vidya* (science of gods).[44] This would point out that apart from study of the *Vedas* and their six branches (*Vedangas*), many other Arts and Sciences were probably compulsorily taught at the *gurukulas*. However, Brahmavidya occupied the pride of place, being called the Paravidya (highest knowledge) as distinct from all others—the Apara Vidyas.[45] So Vaisheshika, Sankhya, Yoga, Nyaya, Mimansa, and Vedanta got included in the syllabus and took the form of Philosophy in later years. In those days even some women had mastery in the subjects of Nyaya, Yoga and Sankhya. We have the example of the exceptionally learned Sulabha in the *Mahabharata*, who had astonished even Dharmadhvaja Janaka by her erudition and extraordinary *yogic* feats.

Kashakritsnani had written a book '*Kashkritsni*' formulating original ideas in Mimansa philosophy, and it was specially studied by women students.[46] We find that in those days there used to be *upadhyayas* (women teachers) as well as distinct from *upadhyayinis* (wives of male teachers). There were even women *acharyas*, who were authorized to teach the Vedas and even perform ***upanayana*** of students. There is evidence that in the time of Panini and Patanjali women used not only to study the *Vedas*, but teach these as well.[47] Cases of women teachers are not rare even as late as 7th and 8th century. There is evidence that when Mandana Mishra on being defeated by Shankaracharya had taken to *sanyasa*, his wife, Ubhayabharati started teaching at ***Shringeri***. It is believed that due to receipt of teaching from Bharati, the lineage at ***Shringeri*** and Dwaraka *mathas* has come to be known as Bharati.[48] In earlier times, we also learn of hostels for women students.[49] Sanskrit was widely studied even in the later days as would be noticed from the reply given by an ordinary maid servant of Mandana Mishra to Shankaracharya in Sanskrit verse. Women had excelled in Medicine and their books have come to light. There is mention of a book written in Sanskrit on midwifery by an Indian woman, Rusa, which was translated in Arabic in 8th century. We also find that teaching of Mathematics to women continued till much later as deduced from the fact that the famous mathematician, Bhaskara II, had written Lilavati in 12th century for teaching his daughter, Lilavati.

Art has continued to occupy a predominant position in the education of women. In Vedic times, education of women was considered incomplete without proficiency in dance. The *Vedas* describe Usha 'as covering herself with gaudy clothes like a girl performing dance.'[50] The tradition continued during the epic period. King Virata had established a dance school in his capital for teaching dance to his daughter, Uttara, and women from the town used to attend the same. Later, we learn of an Art school in the palace of King Agnimitra in 2nd Century B.C. *Malavikagnimitra* speaks of a lady umpire at the test of Malavika in dramatics.[51]

Women excelled in the field of Poetry as well. A number of women of South India, like, Reva, Roha, Madhavi, Anulakshmi, Pahayi, Baddhavahi, Shashiprabha etc. had written excellent poetry in Prakrita. Some of them, like Shilo Bhattarika had earned fame in Sanskrit poetry. Similarly, it is said about Devi Mugdhakari of Gujrat, a great Sanskrit poetess, that due to her artistic poetry in Shringara *rasa* in Lata style, she ever lived in the hearts of poetry lovers.

Likewise, it is said about Vijayanka of Karnataka that she was versatile like Saraswati and had monopoly over Vaidarbhi after Kalidasa. About her Rajashekhara says," It is a mistake that Saraswati has been spoken of as all white, because Vijayanka is dark bluish like a blue lotus." Dr. Altekar had discovered the famous Sanskrit drama written by one Vidya Vajjaka known as '*Kaumudi Mahotsava*'. There are many great poetesses like, Subhadra, Sita, Maruta, Indulekha, Bhavadevi, Vikatanitamba etc. whose works are, however, not available now.

References

1. Rigveda, Purusha Sukta.
2. Manusmiti, 1.31.
3. Gita, 4.13.
4. Gita, 18, 40-46.
5. Raghuvamsha of Kalidasa, 5.24.
6. V.S. Agarwal: Studies in Indian Art, p. 253, Vishwavidyalaya Prakashana, Varanasi.
7. A.S.Altekar: Education in Ancient India
8. Brih. Up. 2.1.
9. Chhandogyopanishad, 5.11.5.
10. Manusmiti., 2.37.
11. *Ibid*, 2.36.
12. Gita, 18.42.
13. *Ibid.*
14. Gita, 8.11 15.
15. Chhandegyopanishad, 6.1.2.
16. Manusmiti., 3.1.
17. Shrimadbhagavata., 1.4.25.
18. Atharavaveda, 12.3.17.18.
19. Harita Bharmashastra
20. P.V. Kane: History of Hindu Dharmashastras, Vol. 2, Pt. 1 p. 294.
21. Ashwalayana Grihyasutra, 3.8.11.

22. Val. Ram., Ayodhya Kanda, 20.15.
23. *Ibid.*, 87.19.
24. Kumarasambhava of Kalidasa 5.16.
25. *Ibid.*
26. Mundakopanishad 3.2.10.
27. Brih.Up., 2.4.3.
28. *Ibid.*, 2.4.5.
29. Uttara Ramachartira of Bhavabhuti, 2.4.
30. *Ibid.*, 2.3.
31. According to Goldstucker and R.K. Bhandarkar, the age of Panini is 7th. century B.C. (Paninikalina Bharata p. 479).
32. Panini Shiksha, 52.
33. Manusmiti., 2.6.7.
34. Rigveda, 10.85.26.
35. Mait. Sam., 4.7.1.
36. Maha. Bh., Sabha Parva, 69.9.
37. *Ibid.*, Vana Parva, 57.14.
38. *Ibid.*, 65.39.
39. Mahabharata, Udyoga Parva, 13.2.8.
40. *Ibid.*, Virata Parva, 21.40-42.
41. *Ibid.*, 20.3-4.
42. Manusmiti., 3.1.
43. Shatapathe Brahmana 11.5.68.
44. Can. Up., 7.1.2.
45. Mundakopanishad, 1.1.4.5.
46. Kashakritsnani had composed a work on Mimansa called Kashakritsni after her. Lady students who went to specialise in it were known as Kashakritsna.-Dr. A.S. Altekar: Education in Ancient India, p. 208.
47. Dr. V.S. Agarwal: Paninikalina Bharaat, p.281.
48. Ramadasa Gaur: Hindutva, Jnanamandal Press, Varanasi.
49. Panini Astadhyayi, 6.2.85.
50. Dr. Altekar : The Position of Women in Ancient India; The Cultural Heritage of India; Shri Ramakrishna Centenary Memorial-, p. 219.
51. Malavikagnimitra, Act 1.

7

Marriage: Types of, its Finality, Age and Characteristics of the Bride and the Groom

Marriage

In ancient times thousands of *brahmacharis* led a life of celibacy and engaged themselves in realization of God, shunning worldly pleasures, but this was not the general picture. It is seen from the *Mahabharata* and the Puranas that in the beginning of creation Prajapati created, through asexual process, sons, Sanatkumaras and Kapila etc. He ordered them to continue the process of creation, but they preferred to remain recluses and Brahma had to create other sons; viz. Marichi, Atri, Angira etc.[1] Continuation of the race was thus at the root of the institution of marriage.

Even if we ignore the desire of the Creator, it will be easy to appreciate that the life of a recluse is not practicable for everyone. Further, such recluses, being far removed from the society and engrossed in contemplation of Brahma, the world would remain deprived of public service. That is why alongwith *nivritti marga*, *pravritti marga* came into being. It is not that in the latter self realization was not the ultimate aim, it is only that it was to go side by side with social service.

Only the *brahmacharis* under the strict discipline of *brahmacharyashrama* could be expected to follow the ideals of marriage and that is why the *Dharmashastra* have enjoined upon them to enter married life. Stress has been laid on sublimation of the common and basic needs of the humans. Marriage was designed to control the most intense desire of all, the sex drive. According to the *Bhagavata*, 'Nobody needs to be told to indulge in sex, meat-eating and drinking. These are but natural to humans. In order to discipline the same marriage, Somayaga, Sautramani *yajnas* have been prescribed. Even so, *kama* without thoughts of the results or *nivritti* are better."[2] In both Vedic and classic literature marriage has been treated as a means for continuance of creation and for attainment of the ideal human state. The teachers used to insist, amongst other things, on need for marriage for continuation of the race in their valedictory address to the students at the end of their education.[3]

The *Smritis* have propounded that the man has to discharge three debts—*devarina, rishirina* and *pitririna*—if he wants to attain *moksha*.[4] This concept leads to a lofty philosophy of life, highlighting need for self-improvement and social service. The way to discharge *devarina* was to perform *daiva karmas*, like *yajnas, rishirina* by acquisition of knowledge, including Vedic studies and spreading the same and *pitririna* by producing worthy children.

Like the *Mahabharata, Manusmrti* also says, "Beget children, do not leave debts for them, arrange for their livelihood, marry off the daughters to able grooms and then lead the life of a recluse in the forests."[5] We know of life long celibates, men and even women, like Sulabha and Shandiya, who followed the path of Brahma. But marriage continued to be treated as the common *dharma* and it was not considered desirable that a woman remained unmarried. The *Mahabharata* narrates the story of daughter of *rishi* Kuni Garga, who having failed to secure a suitable husband, had retired to the forests to perform *tapas* to attain *moksha* and grew quite old in the process. There Narada reprimanded her saying the heaven did not accept an unmarried woman.[6] At this the lady requested the rishis residing in the forest for one of them to take half the fruits of her *tapas* and marry her. This request was accepted by Shringavana with the condition that he would spend only one night with her. This would go to prove that marriage for women came to be regarded as a must in times to come.

Certain anthropologists have opined that in the beginning of civilization sexual relationship had developed without marriage. A confirmation is found in the *Mahabharata*. Unable to have intercourse with his wives due to curse of a *rishi*, Pandu asked Kunti to produce children through *niyoga*. When Kunti objected to this, Pandu quoted an old tradition according to which women were free to have intercourse with other than their husbands as that was the *dharma* in those days. He further clarified that the new tradition was established by Shvetaketu, son of *rishi* Uddalaka, much later. He had got annoyed when he saw a Brahmana grabbing his mother in the presence of his father and wanting to take her away. His father, however, pacified him saying that it was an ancient tradition, wherein women were free to move about like cows. But Shvetaketu was not convinced and he put a stop to this practice in society. It was laid down that sexual relationships out of wedlock were sinful.[7]

The above statement of Pandu could have been based on heresay, for we find Vedic *mantras* replete with eulogization of the institution of marriage much before Shvetaketu. *Rishi* Dirghatama had also laid down the *pativrata dharma* (complete faithfulness to husband), though we do not find therein a direction for the husband also to be compulsorily faithful to the wife.[8]

Types of Marriages

We shall now discuss types of marriages against the above background. The Vedic religion lays down attainment of *svarga* (heaven) through *yajnas* and that the same had to be performed along with the wife. No man without a wife could perform a *yajna*.[9] This provision in the *Taittiriya Brahmana* is being followed in the Hindu society to this day. The only relaxation was that if the wife was not alive or unavoidably absent, the husband could place an image of the wife on his left side and perform the *yajna*. Even Lord Rama had followed this provision, thus bestowing sanctity to the institution of marriage. *Manusmriti* also declares that *grhasthashrama* is the essence of all *ashramas*, which depend on this like all creatures depending on air.[10]

While laying down the lofty ideals of marriage, our *Dharmashastras* did not ignore the gap in intellectual and moral standards in society. That is why lower forms of marriages had also to be recognized. In our culture the ability to hold together has been held to be the chief characteristic of *dharma*.[11] As a via media, our religious leaders classified marriages as desirable, average and outright discardable. That is why in some of the *Grihyasutras*, like Ashvalayana, Apastamba etc., and *Mahabharata*, *Manusmrti* and other *Smrtis* that have classified marriages, we do not come across very high ideals.

The *Smrtis* and the *Mahabharata* have detailed eight types of marriages.[12]

According to the *Manusmriti* these are—*Brahma*, *Daiva*, *Arsha*, *Prajapatya*, *Asura*, *Gandharva*, *Rakshasa* and *Paishacha*.[13] Brahma *vivaha* is the best, in which the groom is invited to the bride's house and the father of the bride hands over the bride to the groom. This is the system mostly in vogue in our country. In the *Daiva vivaha* the priest gives away the bride at the *yajna*. In the *Arsha vivaha* the father of the bride accepts one he-calf and one she-calf from the groom for giving away at the *yajna* before giving away the bride. Some Smrtikaras have decried this system, treating it as *kanyashulka* (bride-price). In the *Mahabharata* Bhishma denounces this by saying that it tantamounts to sale of the bride, the amount of price being immaterial.[14] *Manusmiti* says the same.[15] In the *Prajapatya vivaha* the groom and the bride are simply called upon to act as per *dharma*. In the *Asura vivaha* money is willingly offered to the father of the bride. In the Gandharva *vivaha* the boy and the girl, having taken a liking to each other, take to intercourse and marriage follows later. The marriage of Shakuntala and Dushyanta falls in this category. This marriage was approved by sage Kanva as Dushyanta was known to be a man of character and his attraction to Shakuntala had been at the dictates of his conscience.[16] Most often the girls, even after agreeing to this type of marriage, used to obtain permission from their parents. The *Mahabharata* narrates the story of Tapati, daughter of Surya, who even though agreeing to the proposal of Samvarana for Gadharva *vivaha*, had asked him to obtain permission of her father.[17] In the *Rakshasa vivaha* the girl was forcibly snatched away from her parents against her wish. This was also known as Kshatra *vivaha* as it was prevalent only among the Kshatriyas. The marriages of Rukmini, Amba, Ambika, Ambalika and Subhadra could be classified as midway between *Rakshasa* and Gandharva *vivahas* as they had gone willingly. *Rakshasa vivaha*, however, soon disappeared, being reprehensible. Paishacha *vivaha* was considered the most reprehensible as it involved intercourse with a woman who was asleep or not in senses due to intoxication, in a secluded place where she could not secure help. It may here be clarified that the fact that this *vivaha* was included in the *Smrtis* does not mean that it had their approval; it was there because this system was in vogue at some places. Amongst all types of *vivahas, Manusmrti* approves of only *Brahma, Daiva, Arsha* and *Prajapatya vivahas* for Brahmanas. It, however, permits Rakshasa *vivaha* for Kshatriyas and *Asura vivaha* for Vaishyas and Shudras.[18] *Mahabharata* and *Padma Purana* approve of *Rakshasa* and *Gandharva vivahas* for Kshatriyas.[19] All the same *Brahma vivaha* was always considered the best. The *Dharmashastras* have opined that excellent progeny is born only from the first four *vivahas.*

Love Marriage

The *Gandharva vivaha* became extinct in due course. But in modern times love marriages have sprung up in India due to impact of Western civilization. The so-called highly educated boys and girls, devoid of worldly experience and due to their character formation not having been in accordance with Indian culture, have been settling their marriages secretly, keeping their parents in dark or even against their wish, attracted solely by external appearances and behaviour. The ill effects of this tendency have already started showing up. The external attraction that had brought them together is seen to be wearing off in many cases, resulting in uncongenial living and, in due course, divorce. Even thinkers in Western countries, whose system is being blindly copied here, are alarmed at the growing divorce rate. The Pope has denounced this system and has stressed need for providing moral and religious basis to marriage. It is feared that if blind aping of the West by our youth goes unchecked, the dating system of the West will soon start flourishing here. Only the irresponsible will argue that marriage is a purely personal matter and that there should be unrestricted freedom in this regard. It must be realized that unrestricted freedom needs to be curbed not only for the good of the society, but for the good of the individual himself. It should be remembered that marriage bonds are linked to society and the nation, because the individual has no existence divorced from the society. Realizing this *Manusmiti* prescribed even for the girl to select a suitable match for herself under certain circumstances.[20]

The Finality of Marriage

The highest ideal of marriage is that followed by Parvati. In this once a girl mentally chooses a man to be her husband, she does not even think of marrying anybody else, even if it meant remaining unmarried all her life. Likewise, according to some law makers, marriage was treated as final at the stage of *vakdana* (verbal agreement) itself. As this entailed the most practical problem of bride or groom dying before marriage, a definite requirement—*saptapadi*—was framed by the Smrtikaras. *Manusmrti* lays down that "for wedding chanting of Veda *mantras* of *vivaha* is essential, but the finality of the rite is only after performance of *Saptapadi*."[21] The *Mahabharata* narrates the dispute between Narada and Parvata as to which of the two had the right to marry the daughter of King Sanjaya. The King proposed marriage with Narada, but Parvata objected by saying that he had already taken the girl as his bride. The logic was not accepted and the rule in the *Smriti* was re-iterated that "It is essential to perform *kanyadana* with steadfastness of *manas*, speech and intellect and also to chant Vedic *mantras* of *panigrahana*, but the finality of marriage is achieved only with the performance of *saptapadi*."

Swayamvara

The *Grihyasutras, Manusmriti, Yajnavalkya Smriti* etc. and even *Mahabharata,* do not include *swayamvara* in the list of types of marriages. Even so, the antiquity of this system is unquestioned. There are examples of this practice not only in the pre-historic times, but in the historic period as well. The apparent meaning of *swayamvara* is the practice in which the bride selects the groom herself. But there is hardly any example of such a selection. The practice, however, was that the bride could freely choose her husband within the conditions and limitations prescribed by the father.

The oldest example of *swayamvara,* though a very unusual one, is found in the story of Savitri in the *Mahabharata*. Savitri, on account of her exceptional attainments, had been allowed to roam the earth and choose a husband for herself, but her freedom was limited only to informing her father. Her father, however, agreeing to her choice of Satyavana, performed the marriage accordingly. It must here be remembered that *swayamvara* was not an exhibition or a fair and that the girl was not free to place the *jayamala* around the neck of any youth she liked. The prescribed conditions had to be fulfilled. The *swayamvaras* of Sita, Draupadi, Amba and Ambalika were *viryashulka swayamvaras*, wherein exceptionally difficult conditions for testing strength, bravery, skill, etc. were laid down. Similarly, there used to be *saundarya shulka swayamvaras* at which the bride was free to choose one of the assembled handsome youths. *swayamvaras* of Damayanti and Indumati fall under this category. The last example in the historic age is the *swayamvara* of Sanyogita of Kannauj.

Swayamvara only for Kshatriyas

Swayamvara was not very popular even in ancient times. We find that marriage of Sita's sisters was not as per this practice. So was that of Uttara in Mahabharata period, unlike that of Draupadi. We also do not find evidence of *swayamvara* marriages in other than Kshatriyas. When Arjuna, in the garb of a Brahmana, succeeded in hitting the target, thus earning the right to wed Draupadi, the assembled Kshatriyas had raised a hue and cry that the *swayamvara* was only for the Kshatriyas.[23] The real identity of Arjuna, however, settled the dispute. A statement of Shri Krishna in the *Mahabharata* upholding the same view brought finality to the issue. The *Devi Bhagavata*, too, confirmed the same.[24]

The Ills of *Swayamvara* and its End

The rivalry created amongst the asembled Kshatriya princes at the *swayamvara* used to result in malice and even outright fights, as noticed during *swayamvaras* of Sita and

Draupadi. In the historic period the *swayamvara* of Sanyogita had resulted in a blood bath and a terrible loss of warriors, which was an important factor in the victory of the invader, Mohammad Ghori, over Prithviraja Chauhana. This was the last we hear of *swayamvara*.

The Age of Marriage and the Attributes of the Bride and the Groom

It can not be said for certain that child marriage was non existent in the beginning of civilization. In Vedic times marriage was performed after the *samavartana samskara* at the end of *bahmacharya shrama*, when both the boy and the girl were fully grown up. But there is no clear indication of the minimum age in Vedic literature. Internal evidence, however, goes to indicate that the bride could not be less than sixteen years of age. The *garbhadhana samskara* was prescribed to be performed on the fourth day of marriage, which would show that the bride was certainly ripe for conception. Sushrutacharya, the famous exponent of Ayurveda, has laid down sixteen years as a suitable age of the bride for *garbhadhana*. In due course, with the restriction on Vedic studies for women, the age of marriage for them got lowered. The *Dharmashastras* laid down that the girl must be married off before she started to have menses. Undue stress was laid on this with the result even child marriages became common.

But the *Manusmrti* also laid down that it was better for the daughter remaining unmarried all her life rather than being married to a man devoid of qualities.[25] It has even prescribed Ayurvedic examination of the groom.[26] The *Mahabharata*, too, says that the girl should be married to a person of character, of good deeds and belonging to a noble family. Kalidasa lauds bride and groom of equal qualities.[27]

The provision of a specific age for marriage in the *Smritis* is in regard only to the bride. For the groom, it is after completion of Vedic studies. Much later, in the wake of tyranny over women by various invaders, the tendency to marry them off early gained ground. The age of marriage for the boys also came down due to decline in the practice of *brahmacharya* and study of *Vedas*. The ills of child marriage that followed are only too well known.

In conclusion, let us review the age of marriage of some great women. Savitri had left home in search of a suitable husband. Shakuntala had become pregnant by Gandharva *vivaha*. Damayanti had shown exceptional intelligence in identifying the real Nala amongst the *devas* disguised as Nala. Sukanya had chosen to marry the blind and old *rishi* Chyavana in order to save her father's kingdom. Gandhari had blindfolded herself on hearing that her husband was blind. Kunti had given birth to Karna before marriage. Subhadra had let her love for Arjuna be known before her *harana*. Uttara had conceived immediately after marriage. These examples lead to the unmistakable conclusion that at the time of marriage all these women were not less than fifteen years old when proper conception would be possible. In recent times we have some glaring examples of child marriage; like those of Rani Laksmi Bai, Kasturba Gandhi and Ma Sharada Devi, wife of Ramakrishna Paramahansa, their age at the time of marriage being only thirteen, thirteen and five years respectively. Though child marriage did not hamper their greatness, there are no two opinions regarding its evil effects.

Child marriage did great harm to the Indian society. A general awakening resulted in enactment of Sharda Act, 1929. Though this Act was not very effective in removing this evil, spread of education and changed circumstances are doing away with this practice very fast.

References

1. Mahabharata, Shanti Parva, ch. 339-340, Pt. 3.12.4; Vishnu Purana 1.7.
2. Shrimadbhagavata., 11.5.11.

3. Tait. Up. ShikshaValli, 11.1.2.
4. Manusmiti., 6.35.
5. Maha. Bh., Udyoga Parva, 36.39.
6. Mahabharata, Shalya Parva, 52.12.
7. Mahabharata, Adi Parva, 122.4. 18.
8. *Ibid.*, 104.34.36.
9. Tattariya Brahmana, 2.2.2.6.
10. Manusmiti., 3.77.
11. Mahabharata Karna Parva, 69.58; Shanti Parva, 109-12.
12. Mahabharata, Adi-Sambhava Parva; 73, 8-9.
13. Manusmiti, 3.21.
14. Mahabharata, Anushasana Parva, 45.20.
15. Manusmiti., 3.53.
16. Shakuntala, 1.21.
17. Mahabharata, Adi Parva, 174-20.
18. Manusmiti., 3.24.
19. Padma Purana, 1.40.
20. Manusmiti., 9.90-92.
21. *Ibid.*, 8. 227.
22. Mahabharata, Drona Parva, 55.15.16.
23. Mahabharata, 189.7.
24. Devi Bhagavata, 3-18.41.
25. Manusmiti., 9.89.
26. Mahabharata, Anushasana Parva, 44.3.
27. Shakuntala, 5.16.

8

Ideals of Marriage: Monogamy and *Pativratya* (Faithfulness to the Husband)

In the appraisal of ideals of marriage a question naturally arises as to what the duties laid down for the husband towards the wife are. But while doing so it should be remembered that in the Indian culture adherence to one's prescribed duties was not conditional and not dependent on what others did or did not do. During the *vanavasa*, Draupadi, doubting divine justice, once exclaimed – "How is it that Duryodhana engrossed in the path of injustice is enjoying and Dharmaraja Yudhishthira, even though unwavering in the path of *dharma*, is facing all sorts of trouble!" To this Yudhishthira had replied "I do not barter *dharma*. I follow the rules of *dharma* rigidly, because I consider it my duty to do so." This basic thinking was at the root of *pativrata dharma*. The wife remained steadfast to the husband irrespective of what he did. But it did not mean there was a license to the husband to follow evil ways, while expecting his wife to be ideal like Sita and Savitri. Shvetaketu has laid down faithful behaviour for both husband and wife.[1] This is why faithful husband and wife both have been eulogized in our culture. This also rejects the theory of scholars, like Thomas, that monogamous society was foreign to Indian concept.[2] Even so, it will have to be admitted that same stress was not laid on monogamy as on *pativratya*. That is why the number of great men steadfastly devoted to their wives is seen to be limited, whereas *pativratas* are galore.

The *Shastras* have approved of more than one marriage for a man, if needed for the birth of a son. But in actual practice this provision was mostly misused by men. Similarly, whereas *Dharmashastras* permitted a male divorcee to remarry for the sake of performance of religious rites, widow remarriage was forbidden. Viewed against this background, those men, who never thought of marrying again even on the death of the wife, did deserve praise. The earliest amongst the *ekapatnivratas* (devoted to the wife) was Nala, who had remained steadfast to his wife, Damayanti, against all odds.[3] It is also well known that Lord Rama, instead of marrying again, had got a golden statue of Sita set up next to him for the performance of the *ashwamedha yajna*. The *Bhagavata* records that 'Rama Chandra followed *ekapatnivrata*, like *rajarshis*, and set an example for others.'[4] We further find that Lord Rama had made it a habit to consult Sita in all important matters. The ideal man-wife relationship is summarized in *Valmikiya Ramayana*, wherein Rama says, " In performance of duties my beloved wife is like a *dasi* (servant); in affection, like mother; in forgiveness, like *prithivi*; in intimate matters, like Rambha and in recreation, like a friend."

Kalidasa narrates how Aja had eulogized the qualities of Indumati in more or less similar words.[5] Bhasa has praised the wife as a consort, minister, friend and a close relation all in one. The *Shatapatha Brahmana* says that "till a man takes a wife, his *atman* is only half. That becomes complete when he begets a child after marriage."[6] The *Smritis* and *Dharmashastras* have followed this Vedic dictum. Apastamba says that "both husband and wife are co-sharers in the religious rites and in the outcome of their good deeds; so much so that they do not have separate shares in property."[7] The *Padma Purana* says that "if husband and wife live in harmony, there is no greater heaven than that."[8] *Manusmriti* has directed that "the husband and the wife must be true to each other throughout their lives and that if they have to live apart, even then their actions should not be opposed to each other."[9] The Puranas have rightly declared that if the husband and wife are congenial to each other, *dharma, artha, kama,* all three are realized.[10] The Vedic dictum that the wife is a *sakha* (companion) was followed literally in the later literature. The *Mahabharata* says, "the wife is man's *sakha* and the son is his *atma*."[11] *Brahmanas;* like, *Taittiriya* (3.3.3.5), *Shatapatha* (5.2.1.10), *Aitareya* and *Gopatha* all declare that the man is incomplete without the wife. The Mahabharata, stressing the inevitability of the wife says, "The householder may be surrounded by sons, grandsons, daughters-in-law and servants, still the house is empty without the wife."[12] It further says that the wife is a sure remedy for all ills,[13] and that the house without the wife should be treated a forest.[14] That the husband repents for ill treatment of the wife is highlighted by Kalidasa. He writes that Dushyanta due to the curse of a *rishi* had forgotten that he had entered into *Gandharva vivaha* with Shakuntala. Later, when he was absolved of that curse and the memory of the *vivaha* had returned, he fell on her feet and repented profusely.[15]

The *Mahabharata* says that "the husband is called *bharta* (provider) because he looks after her. If he does not do so, neither he is her *bharta* nor her husband."[16] Kautilya in his *Arthashastra* has even prescribed punishment for a person taking to *sanyasa* without providing for his wife and children satisfactorily. Apastamba has prescribed that "a man, misbehaving with his wife is a *dravyatikrami* and has to spend six months wearing an ass skin and begging alms."[17] *Manusmiti* also enjoins upon both husband and wife to be faithful to each other.[18]

Pativratya

The concept of *Pativratya* is unique in Indian culture. The *Vedas* have given position of equality to both husband and wife, and both are considered half and half of the *atman*. At the time of *panigrahana* the husband and wife jointly pray that 'Vishvadevas and Varuna may join our hearts and Matarishva, Dhata and Deshtri may bind us together.'[19] The lofty ideal of relationship between the man and wife continues in Indian culture, with the *pativratas* occupying an honoured and even revered position.

Some scholars feel that the women have lost their freedom of movement etc. enjoyed by them in Vedic times due to undue stress on *pativratya* subsequently. But this is not so, as even the Rigvedic *mantras* chanted at the time of marriage point to the basis for *pativratya*.[20] The post Vedic literature shows that the *pativratas* acquired still greater position in society. According to *Manusmrti*, "a woman, who controlling her *manas*, speech and body, never behaves in opposition to her husband, gains *patiloka* after death and in the world she is hailed as *sadhvi* (great soul)." He further propounds that "even if the husband is devoid of morality and good qualities, a *sadhvi* woman must serve him like a god. She does not have to perform *yajnas, vratas* and *upavasas* (fast) separately from her husband and becomes entitled to heaven through service alone of the husband. She must not think of harming her husband, even after his death. The widow must not think of another man and must spend the rest of her life on meagre vegetarian diet." The provisions laid down by Manusmiti for an ideal *pativrata* have been corroborated by Smritikaras; like, Yajnavalkya, *Mahabharata, Valmikiya Ramayana* and many *Puranas*. Goswami Tulasidasa has spread the ideal of a *pativrata* as enjoined by *Smritis* etc. amongst crores of Hindus. The preaching of *pativrata dharma* by Anusuya to Sita, described in the *Rama Charita Manasa*, is a true symbol of Indian tradition.[22] In praise of *pativratas*, the *Mahabharata* says that

Lakshmi herself has declared that she dwells in them.[23] The greatness of *pativratas* has been praised even by non-Aryans. Amir Khusro, the famous poet, says that nobody can match the Hindu women in the path of love, because they even burn themselves on the funeral pyre of the husband. The *pativratas* can be classified in two. In one case, having once mentally selected a man as husband, the woman would not marry another man under any circumstances, even if it meant remaining an unmarried *brahmacharini*. The others are those who followed *pativratya* after marriage. We shall give some well known examples of both types.

Parvati

She had resolved to secure Mahadeva as her husband and performed severe *tapas* to this end. As is well known, she did not give up her resolve in spite of dissuasion by Saptarshis, who enumerated many so-called vices of Shiva and praised Vishnu profusely. Parvati rebuffed them saying that she would go on trying for Shiva as husband, even if it meant remaining unmarried for crores of lives.[24] Subsequently, Saptarshis, in order to test her again, told her that Shiva had burnt down Kamadeva and so marriage was out of question for him. To this Parvati told them, "you think Shiva was full of *kama* so far and has burnt Kamadeva only now. But I have always known him to be the greatest *yogi*, untouched by *kama*."[25]

Savitri

Due to her exceptional brilliance King Ashvapati had allowed his daughter, Savitri, to roam around the world and select a suitable husband for herself. In her quest she came across Satyavana, who was living with his father, *rajarshi* Dyumatsena in a hermitage, mentally selected him as her husband and informed her father accordingly. The story goes that Narada appeared and tried to dissuade her saying that Satyavana was destined to live for only one year more. But she replied, 'Distribution of property is done only once and the daughter is given away only once. So whether Satyavana is to live long or not, whether he is full of virtues or not, since I have accepted him as my husband, the question of choosing somebody else simply does not arise.'[26] Seeing her resolve her father married her to Satyavana. Savitri, giving up princely life, started living with Satyavana as a hermit. It is well known how she was able to impress Yamaraja to spare him when his time had come after a year. That is why even now women desirous of long life for their husbands observe *batasavitri vrata* and '*Savitri bhava*' has become an accepted form of blessing for young girls.

Damayanti

Nala, son of king 'Virasena of Nishadha and Damayanti, daughter of king Bhima of Vidarbha, were considered to be epitomes of beauty. Both came to know of each other and fell deeply in love. Finding that Damayanti was languishing in love, her father arranged *swayamvara* for her. Even gods were keen to win her, but finding that she had already set her mind on Nala, some gods, Indra, Varuna, Agni and Yama played a trick. At the *swayamvara* they all acquired the form of Nala and seated themselves amongst the kings and princes. But Damayanti was very sharp. She knew of some secret identification for gods and was able to recognize Nala. She ignored the gods and placed the garland around Nala's neck.

The story goes that in due course Nala lost his entire kingdom in games of dice to his wily brother, Pushkara, who banished both Nala and Damayanti with just meagre clothes on. Out of Pushkara's fear nobody in the kingdom ventured to give them shelter. As a result, they had to undergo all sorts of tribulations, remaining without food for days on end. Nala tried to convince Damayanti to leave him and go to her parents, but as an ideal wife she refused.

Ultimately one night, finding Damayanti fast asleep, Nala left her for an unknown destination. His idea was that finding herself alone, Damayanti would go to her parents. But Damayanti was so disconsolate about the plight of Nala that she started wandering in search of Nala. In the process she got sucked into the coils of a python, but a hunter saved her life by killing the python. The hunter was a wicked person and he tried to rape the lady. But as per the narrative in the *Mahabharata*, he dropped dead due to effectiveness of Damayanti's *pativrata*.[27]

In the course of her determined search, Damayanti reached the capital of king of Chedi, Subahu, whose mother gave her shelter in the palace. In the meantime spies of king Bhima located her there and brought her to her parents' place. But Damayanti forsook all worldly pleasures and lived like a recluse. Nala had, in his wanderings, found the job of a charioteer with the king of Ayodhya, Rituparna, under the pseudonym of Bahuka. The spies of king Bhima, who were looking for Nala, heard of Bahuka's unusual skill as a charioteer. Even though Nala had lost his handsomeness, they were convinced that Bahuka was no other than Nala himself, as the latter was known far and wide for his excellence in this art. The spies gave the news to king Bhima. Bhima thought of a ruse and sent a message to king Rituparna to attend *swayamvara* of Damayanti next day, the idea being that only Nala could drive the chariot fast enough to be in time. The ruse worked and Nala was thus located. Subsequently Nala was able to defeat Pushkara at the dice game, winning back his kingdom. The story of Damayanti is a burning example of *pativrata*.

Sukanya

Sukanya, daughter of king Sharyati, was extremely beautiful and compassionate. Once *maharshi* Chyavana was in such a profound and prolonged *samadhi* in a forest that his body got fully covered with termites and became totally unrecognizable, only two bright objects remaining visible in place of eyes. One day Sukanya, along with her friends, happened to be there and out of curiosity she thrust two thorns in the burning eyes. The sage lost his eyesight and his *samadhi* was broken. Even though the sage did not express any anger, there was a heavenly retribution and the natural activities of urination and defecation of all humans, and even animals, in the kingdom came to a stop. King Sharyati took it to be the result of some grave sin in the kingdom and soon came to know that some one had blinded the sage Chyavana. On coming to know this, Sukanya told the whole incident to her father.

Sharyati went to the sage and pleaded forgiveness for the sin committed unknowingly by his daughter. The sage took mercy and said, "I have not cursed anybody and with my blessings you all will, no doubt, be happy. But you will have to give to me in marriage that daughter of yours who has made me blind. The king was in a fix and could not decide. Sukanya soon came to know of the king's dilemma and immediately made up her mind, as she could not bear the misery she had caused to the entire kingdom by her folly. She thought nothing of giving up royal splendour and spending the whole life with a blind old man. She prevailed upon the king to marry her off to the sage.

Sukanya started living as a devoted wife, looking after the sage without caring for her own needs. Once it so happened that while Sukanya was bathing in a lake, the Ashwinikumaras, who were epitomes of beauty, appeared there and tried to seduce her. She tried to remind them of their godly status and to desist, but in vain. She threatened to burn them down with a curse. On this the Ashwinikumaras were immensely pleased as they were only testing her *pativratya*. They started treating the sage, who not only got back his eyesight but his youth as well.

Gandhari

Gandhari was the daughter of king Subala of Gandhara. He married her off to blind king Dhritarashtra due to pressure of Bhishma Pitamaha. She had been brought up in the tradition of *pativratas*. She decided to blindfold herself lifelong, as she felt that the wife should not enjoy what her husband was unable to do. Even Lord Krishna, while begging forgiveness on behalf of the Pandavas at the end of the *Mahabharata* war, told her, "O Great Soul! Your sacrifice is so great that if you desire you can open your eyes and the anger in the same can burn down the entire earth."[28]

The *pativratya* of Draupadi has been praised not only by the Pandavas, but by *pativratas*, like Kunti and Gandhari, and by Krishna, Veda Vyasa, Bhishma and Vidura. When Yudhishthira had lost her at the dice game, she had raised a pertinent question before the court as to whether Yudhishthira could have wagered her after he had lost himself. Even a wise man like Bhishma was unable to give a satisfactory answer. Even then in the tradition of *pativratas*, Draupadi did not question the judgment of Yudhishthira and only turned to Lord Krishna to save her honour.

It was Draupadi's *pativratya* that saved her from the evil designs of Jayadratha during the *vanavasa* and from Virata's brother-in-law, Kichaka, during the *ajnatavasa*. She was able to keep all five husbands pleased, which made Satyabhama, consort of Krishna, ask her what mantra she used to be able to do so. Draupadi chided her saying that it was not as a result of some *mantra*, but due to meticulous adherence to *pativratya*. Her discourse to Satyabhama about the duties of a *pativrata* is the crux of *pativratya*.[29]

Amba

Bhishma defeated all the assembled kings at the *swayamvara* of Amba, Ambika and Ambalika, daughters of king of Kashi and forcibly carried them away to Hastinapura for marrying them to his step-brothers. There Amba told Bhishma that she had mentally selected Shalvaraja to be her husband, whereupon Bhishma sent her to the latter. But Shalvaraja rejected her saying that she was no longer *ananyapurva* (not belonging to anybody else). Amba chose to remain unmarried lifelong and to take revenge from Bhishma. The story is well known as to how she avenged herself in the next birth as Shikhandi. This shows to what extent the determination of a *pativrata* can go.

Sita

The *Valmikiya Ramayana* and the Ramacharita Manasa have highlighted the *pativratya* of Sita very vividly. Sita thought nothing of the hardships of spending fourteen years in forests in exile with Rama. She was so clear in her understanding of duties of a *pativrata* that she paid no heed to pleadings from all sides, including husband Rama, to give up her resolve. While explaining the duties of a *pativrata*, Anusuya, a great *pativrata* herself, had praised her profusely.[30] Sita has herself narrated how she was alive to the lofty ideals of *pativratya* in her day-to-day dealings.[31]

Later, when Ravana forcibly took her away, she would never succumb to his entreaties, nor was she scared of his powers. She not only castigated him for his sinful act, but even insulted him by contrasting with the great Rama. She declared, " Put me in prison or tear me into pieces. I have no attachment to this body or life."[32] It was certainly her unflinching devotion to Rama and her *pativratya* that she was able to survive the torture.

In spite of her unquestioned devotion, she had no complaint when Rama asked her to prove her innocence by entering into the fire. Nor did she utter a word of protest when she was exiled subsequently. Her message to Rama was, "What I am suffering is the result of sins of past lives.

I shall certainly protect my life, not because I want to live, but because I am carrying your *tejas* in my womb. My only desire is that I may get you as a husband in my future lives." The concept of *pativratya* that originated in the *Vedas* and spread through the *Ramayana, Mahabharata*, Smritis and *Puranas* and which was symbolized by the great souls, like Parvati, Arundhati, Sita etc. is a unique contribution to Indian culture. Some people are, however, critical of the provision that the wife must remain faithful to the husband even if he is lame, blind, dumb and even characterless. The argument against this is that it is the human duty to serve the helpless and those of weak resolve. The Buddha personally nursing a leper and Kasturba carrying the urine and stool of guests at her husband's bidding are too well known examples.

The Power of *Pativratya*

There are many instances of *pativratas* endowed with supernatural powers like profound *yogis*. There is a story in the *Mahabharata* of a learned Brahmana named Kaushika who was made to realize the insignificance of his learning and *tapas* by an ordinary woman. She was so much engrossed in her duties towards her needy husband that she was inattentive to this Brahmana at her door. When she was taken up for this, she told him that she was not a *balaka* (a bird) who could be burnt down merely by his angry gaze. She knew, through the miraculous power of *pativratya*, that the Brahmana had burnt down a *balaka* for inadvertently sitting on his head merely by his angry gaze. We also know of the earth splitting in two on the request of Sita to engulf her. Likewise, at the end of the *Mahabharata* war the Pandavas were unable to face Gandhari for fear of a curse.[34] Even Krishna could not escape Gandhari's curse when she told him, "You could have stopped the war, if you had so desired. So due to your guilt the Vrishnis will fight off to a finish and you will also have a sad end.

Krishna, in order to honour the word of a *pativrata* had accepted the curse, which came true literally. Much earlier, Damayanti had burnt down the vicious hunter as narrated earlier. These are just some typical examples.

Pativratya and Individuality

An erroneous feeling has been gaining ground that *pativratya* kills individuality and that a *pativrata* becomes a puppet in the hands of her husband. It must be clearly remembered that a *pativrata* is not one who feigns faithfulness to the husband out of fear or dependence or fear of social stigma. But when the wife out of her own free will considers it her paramount duty to serve her husband with *manas*, speech and action and merges her wishes with those of her husband, how could it be termed slavery of the husband? *Pativratya* is the sum total of righteous determination, fortitude, and pointed devotion, qualities which make a man truly great and a woman, perfect.

Even in historical times we know how Yashodhara had given up all royal comforts on hearing of her husband, the Buddha's renunciation. We also know how Kasturba had followed all her life in the footsteps of her husband, Mahatma Gandhi, regardless of discomforts arising many a time. Her greatness is clear from her refusal to accept Presidentship of the All India Congress in 1923 saying, "The honour enjoyed by Mahatmaji is also my honour. No honour can be greater to me than the fact that Mahatmaji is my husband." Surely, none of these women had lost their individuality.

References

1. Mahabharata, Adi Parva 122-16.19.
2. P. Thomas: Women throughout the Ages, p. 302.
3. Mahabharata,Vana Parva, 64.17.
4. Shrimadbhagavata. Skandha 9.10-55.

5. Raghuvamsha of Kalidasa, 8.52-67.
6. Shatapatha Brahmana, 5.16.10.
7. Ap. Dh. Sut.
8. Padma Purana, Uttara Khanda 223.56.7.
9. Manusmiti. 9.101.102.
10. Markandeya Purana, 67.71.
11. Mahabharata , Adi Parva 374.73.
12. *Ibid.*, 12.144.5.
13. *Ibid.*, 3.58.29.
14. *Ibid.*,12.144,6..
15. Shakuntala, 7.24.
16. Mahabharata, Shanti Parva, 57,44.45.
17. Ap.Dh. Sut. 1.9.18.
18. Manusmiti.,9.101.
19. Rigveda 10.85.47.
20. Rigveda, 10.10.14.
21. Manusmiti., 5,154-157.
22. Ramacharita Manasa. Aranya Kanda.
23. Maha. Bh., Anushasana Parva, 11-14.
24. Ramacharita Manasa, Balakanda.
25. *Ibid.*
26. Maha. Bh., Vana Parva 294.26.2.
27. Mahabharata, Vana Parva 63.39.
28. Mahabharata, Shalya Parva 63.65.
29. Mahabharata, Vana Parva 233.10-49.
30. Val. Ra., Ayodhya Kanda, 117.22-29.
31. *Ibid.*, 117.
32. *Ibid.*, Aranya Kand, 47.
33. Raghuvamsha of Kalidasa, 14.62.
34. Mahabharata, Shalya Parva, 63-65.
35. *Ibid.*, 63-65.

9

Polyandry, Polygamy, *Anuloma* and *Pratiloma Vivahas*

Polyandry

Polyandry could never take roots in a culture which prized *pativratya,* but there are certain exceptions. The most well known case is that of marriage of Draupadi. As it was both against *shastras* and tradition, it needs to be analysed.

When Bhima and Arjuna came back from the *svayamvara* with Draupadi, they shouted from outside the cottage itself, "Mother, we have brought the alms." This was nothing unusual as the Pandavas used to go out daily and bring home alms. In the normal way, Kunti spoke from inside itself, "Distribute amongst all you brothers." Now, when they entered the cottage, Kunti was in a fix. Yudhishthira being an acknowledged knower of *dharma,* was asked by the mother to find a way out in keeping with *dharma.* He, considering all aspects, decreed that Draupadi should marry all the brothers. The logic behind this decision was that since the mother held a higher position than the father and even *acharya,* her word had to be honoured at all cost. Another reason given by Yudhishthira was that the dictates of conscience had also to be honoured. Sceptics may say that voice of conscience is the best subterfuge for acting in a particular way. But in case of a person like Yudhishthira, who symbolized *dharma* itself, voice of conscience could certainly not go wrong. In later times,

Kalidasa is seen to be stating in *Abhijnana Shakuntalam* that in case of doubt, the righteous should turn to the voice of conscience.[1] Here Yudhishthira narrates two incidents. One was the marriage of a woman, Jatila, with seven *rishis*, and the other, that of Vakshi with ten brothers. He also considered this in keeping with the family tradition. Though we do not find an indication of any such tradition in the *Mahabharata*, Vaidya has opined that 'this custom was prevalent amongst early Chandravamshis who had initially come down from the Himalayas.'[2] We do find such a custom prevailing to this day in Jaunsar Bawar and Kinnaur in the Himalayas, but we can not be sure of the Chandravamshis having come from the Himalayas. Only because Pandu had lived for sometime in the Himalayas and Pandavas were born there, they could not be considered as hailing from that region. Rather, they and Kauravas both had descended from Bharata who had ruled over North Indian plains. It thus seems that the views of Vaidya are based on conjecture. We also know that Drupada, father of Draupadi, was not convinced with the views of Yudhishthira and the matter ended only when *maharshi* Vedavyasa appeared and revealed that Draupadi's marriage to five husbands had been pre-ordained. However, the above narrative would establish that polyandry was not the norm, rather an exception. Even Vedavyasa has called polyandry *amanusha*, i.e., not for humans.

The Pandavas had framed very rigid rules for success of the marriage, which was possible only for a very extra-ordinary woman like Draupadi to follow. One of the rules was that if Draupadi was alone with some Pandava, and another one entered, he would have to go in exile for twelve years. The story goes that once Arjuna, in order to rush to the help of a Brahmana, had to enter the room of Yudhishthira for collecting his arms. At that time he was alone with Draupadi. Consequently, Arjuna had to go in exile for twelve years, in spite of the fact that breach of the rule was for a noble cause.

According to Rahul Sankrityayan, Kinnaur remained under Tibetan rule till 8th century AD and the practice of polyandry in Tibet was passed on to it due to this contact.[4] It is likely that this practice was adopted by Jaunsar Bawar also due to ancient trade contacts with Tibet.

Polygamy

We find evidence of polygamy even in vedic times. The story of Pururava in the Rigveda indicates that he had several wives. The *Ramayana*, the *Mahabharata* and *Puranas* mention polygamy even by many important persons. Even a great sage, like, Yajnavalkya had two wives—Maitreyi and Katyayani. The religious provision that no *yajna* could be performed without a wife, and the belief that only a son could prevent the father from going to *naraka* (hell), appear to be the basic reasons for prevalence of polygamy. Nevertheless, in spite of the high examples set by Rama, Nala etc. the evil practice has been continuing on one pretext or other. An Act has, however, been passed after Independence, which will be dealt with later.

Savarna and *Asavarna* (*Anuloma* and *Pratiloma*) *Vivahas*

In vedic times a Brahmana could marry a Kshatriya and vice versa. But there is no clear indication whether all *varnas* could inter-marry. The above limited inter-marriages could be called *anuloma* and *pratiloma vivahas*. This nomenclature, not known in Vedic times, seems to have come with the growth of a plethora of castes within the four *varnas*. The term *pratiloma* occurring in the Vedic literature, however, means 'contrary to established custom'. King Ajatashatru, who had profound knowledge of Brahma, on being requested by the learned Brahmana, Dripta Balaki, to clarify certain doubts said, " It is *pratiloma* for a Brahmana to ask a Kshatriya about Brahma."[5]

In due course, when these terms got to be used in the context of marriage, *anuloma vivaha* came to mean a marriage between a Brahmana groom and a bride of the other three *varnas,* between a Kshatriya groom and a bride of Vaishya or Shudra *varna* or between a Vaishya groom and a Shudra bride. *Pratiloma* meant marriage of a Kshatriya, Vaishya or Shudra groom with a bride of a higher *varna.* Typical examples of *anuloma vivaha* are those of *rishis* like, Kardama, Chyavana, Shyavashva, Kakshivana and Vimada, who had married Kshatriya brides. In the *Ramayana* we find marriage of Shanta, daughter of King Dasharatha, with *rishi* Rishyashringa. There are some Vedic examples of *pratiloma vivaha,* too, in the limited sense. Shashvati, daughter of *rishi.* Angirasa, was married to king Asanga. *rishi* Shukracharya's daughter, Devayani, was married to king Yayati.

In due course *pratiloma vivahas* ceased entirely. By the *Mahabharata* time, even *anuloma vivaha* was discouraged. The last socially accepted *anuloma vivaha* appears to be the one between the Brahmana king Agnimitra and the Kshatriya bride Malavika in the Shunga period. Thereafter, with the proliferation of castes the rules of marriage became rigid and only *savarna vivahas* got social approval. The *Manusmriti* had given a definite directive that 'the *dvijas* must marry only *savarna* girls.'[6] It was finally declared in both *Manusmriti* and *Yajnavalkya Smriti* that 'marriage should be between *savarnas* only. If it had to be performed between *asavarnas,* it must not be with *panigrahana mantras.*'[6] The wife of an *asavarna* marriage had no right to perform religious rites alongwith the husband. As a result, both *anuloma* and *pratiloma vivahas* vanished in due course.

The main reason for prohibiting *anuloma* and *pratiloma vivahas* was the anxiety to preserve purity of the race. Hundreds of castes had sprung up even by the *Mahabharata* time. This would be clear from the famous dialogue between the python and Yudhishthira, where the latter says. "It has become difficult to establish the *varna* from birth, because there are too many hybrid castes."[7] The concern of the elders in those days would be evident from the fact that Arjuna wanted to avoid the war fearing that large scale killings would lead to proliferation of hybrid castes.[8]

At present, however, with the passage of The Hindu Marriage Act, 1955 there are no obstacles in intercaste marriages. We shall revert to this topic later.

References

1. Shakuntala, 1.21.
2. Mahabharata Mimamsa, p. 229-230 : C.V.Vaidya (translated by Madhava Rao Sapre).
3. Mahabharata, Adi Parva, 2.117.
4. Rahul Sankrityayan: 'Kinnara Desha Mein' p. 301.
5. Brih. Kaushitaki Brah. Upanishad, 4.18.
6. Manusmiti. 3.43.
7. Mahabharata, Vana Parva 180.31.
8. Gita, 1.42.

10
Widow Remarriage and *Niyoga*

Widow Remarriage

We do not find evidence of widow remarriage in the Vedic literature. The *Mahabharata* and *Manusmriti* declare, "The share in a partition is determined once for all. That I shall give away something is spoken only once and the daughter is given away in marriage only once."[1] The *Manusmriti* argues that 'in marriage chanting of Vedic *mantras* of *panigrahana* is a must and that these *mantras* are applicable to a *kanya* (unmarried daughter) only. Therefore, such religious rites are not for the widows.[2] It further says "A widow must not think of remarriage and must spend rest of her life in piety as a *brahmacharini*. A pious widow attains heaven, even if she has no son."[3] The *Yajnavalkya Smriti*[4] completely agrees with the *Manusmriti*.

However, a particular *shloka* in another *Smriti* and *Agni Purana*[5] appears to sanction widow remarriage under certain circumstances. But most scholars hold that this *shloka* has been misinterpreted. They hold that these conditions apply to a woman whose *vagdana* (engagement) only has been performed and *panigrahana* and *saptapadi* are yet to be performed. It is only if the male dies during the interregnum, the so-called widow could remarry. This view carries weight and thus it is doubtful whether this *Smriti* supports widow remarriage. The cases of widow remarriage are rare in our history. In case of Tara, Sugriva had taken her as a kept on death of Bali and there was no remarriage. It appears that the widows in those days were not in a pitiable state as in later times, or else the society would have sanctioned widow remarriage.

However, a discussion of widow remarriage based only on *Smritis* would be incomplete. The problem of widows in the changing society did call for solutions. In due course, the pernicious custom of child marriage definitely swelled the number of widows. We can also not deny that the Hindu society, during later centuries, has inflicted extreme tortures on widows in the name of ideals of womanhood. Even though an integral part of the family, the widow is constantly reminded of her widowhood. Being considered inauspicious, she is to remain isolated on occasions of rejoicing, like a marriage. If she inherits property, she is even in danger of her life, so much so that many a Hindu widow is forced to leave the house and take to a life of immorality for a living or to get converted.

The widow problem has been attracting attention of not only social reformers, but even traditionalists. The latter have, however, been too scared to go against the established norms. Even the great social reformer, Swami Vivekananda, did not clearly support widow remarriage and confined himself only to deprecation of child marriage. It appears that the first to address himself squarely to this problem was Raja Ram Mohan Roy. But it was the tireless efforts of Ishwara Chandra Vidyasagara and Swami Dayananda Saraswati which made a real dent. Vidyasagara was instrumental in getting the Hindu Widow Remarriage Act, 1856 passed. Swamiji propagated widow remarriage through the Arya Samaj. Both were erudite Vedic scholars and used to quote the Vedas in support of their stand.

But due to the age-old tradition of *pativratya* and *sati dharma* ingrained in the society, even the women who were the sufferers continued to be reluctant to take to widow remarriage. In spite of the law and the Press and the Platform, the progress has been slow, but the opposition is certainly disappearing. Similarly, the Sharda Act has not seen the end of child marriage and *vigorous social* reform is called for. Lastly, as even the *Dharmashastras* have provided for enacting *apaddharmas* (exceptions to the rule) as demanded by changing times, widow remarriage cannot be said to be against the *Smritis* in the present age.

Niyoga

Niyoga is a technical term in the *dharmashastra* which denotes a process in which if the husband died issueless or he was physically incapable of producing a child, the wife or the widow could take the help of a near relative to do so. But though cases of *niyoga* do find a mention in the *Mahabharata* and in earlier times, this could not assume the form of a custom. Some scholars[6,7,8] quote two *mantras* of the *Rigveda* in support of *niyoga*, which *mention* cases of Purukutsani, Purandhri Vaddhrimati and Vimada; there are others who hold that these *mantras* are not in the context of *niyoga*.

But the question remains as to how an obviously reprehensible act like *niyoga* could find place in a culture in which highest ideals of *pativratya* and marriage had got entrenched. Maybe, the exhortation in the *Taittiriya Upanishad* -'*prajatantum ma vyachhetsih*'(do not let the family line disappear[9] and '*aputrasya gatirnasti*' (one without a son can not go to heaven)' —was at the root of this aberration. As begetting a son was considered a religious obligation, *niyoga* might have been thought of as a via media. But the rules in this regard were very strict. One was that when the possibility of the husband producing a child became nil, the wife could enter into intercourse with the younger brother of the husband or with one who belonged to the same *pinda*, but only with the approval of the husband or the elders.[10] Further, "the man should cover himself with ghee and enter into intercourse at night, keeping strict control over his tongue and with the sole interest of producing a child."[11] Also, after the *niyoga*, the woman and the man must start behaving like a daughter-in-law and the guru.[12] And, "if the man and the woman involved in niyoga enter into it with the idea of satiation of passion, they bring upon them the sin of entering into liaison with the daughter-in-law or the wife of the *guru*."[13]

The opinion of the *Manusmriti* is contained in the dictum—"The widow of a *dwijati* must not enter into niyoga with anybody, because this is against the *sanatana dharma*.[14] It claims, "The Vedic *vivaha mantras* nowhere mention *niyoga* or widow remarriage."[15]

The incidents of *niyoga* quoted above are not established beyond doubt. But the *Mahabharata* does quote examples which prove existence of *niyoga* prior to *Mahabharata* times. It is well known that Satyavati and Bhishma had persuaded Vyasa to perform *niyoga* due to Vichitravirya being issueless, thus presenting the spectre of end of the Kuruvamsha. Similarly, when issueless Pandu requested Kunti to produce a child through *niyoga*, she had refused at first and Pandu had to quote the ancient example of *niyoga* by Damayanti, Queen of Saudasa, with Vasishtha to produce son Ashmaka.[16] The example of these Kuru women would go to show that in spite of religious provisions the process of *niyoga* was not wholly acceptable to women, in general.

The reluctance of women and the impracticability of the provisions seem to have led to discontinuation of the system. *Brihaspati Smriti* says,"No doubt, *Manu* has talked of *niyoga*, but he has also disapproved of it. This is because whereas people established in virtue during the *satyayuga* and the *tretayuga* could do so, it was not possible for the sensual people in the later ages to observe the rigid rules of *niyoga*."[17] The happenings in the reign of Vena, which saw unbridled sexual behavior and *niyoga*, must certainly have led the leaders of society to declare *niyoga* to be *pashudharma.*[18] Manu, Brihaspati etc. banished *niyoga* for ever from the society.

References

1. Mahabharata,Vana Parva 294.26.
2. Manusmiti., 9.47.
3. Manusmiti., 5.156-160.
4. Yaj. Smriti, *vivaha* chapter.
5. Agni Purana, 154.5.6.
6. V.S. Upadhyaya: Women in Rigveda.
7. Rigveda 4.42.8.9.
8. P. V. Kane: History of Hindu Dharmashastra, Bk 2, Pt. i.
9. Tattaiyopanishad, Shiksha Valli.1.11.1.
10. Manusmriti.,9.58.
11. *Ibid.*, 9.60.
12. *Ibid.*, 9.62.
13. *Ibid.*, 9.63.
14. *Ibid.*, 9.64.
15. *Ibid.*, 9.65.
16. Mahabharata Adi Parva 122.21.22.
17. Brih. Sm.
18. Manusmriti., 9.66-68.

11
The Custom of *Sati*

The custom of *sati* seems to be rooted in high ideals of *pativratya.* Its purpose would be clear from the statement of Sita while entreating Rama to take her to the forests with him that "I may have you as my husband in the next life as well. The wise have said that once a woman is given away by *kanyadana* by her father, she continues to be the wife of her husband even after death."[1] The ideals of *pativratya* laid down that the relationship between the husband and the wife continued in the after life as well. The result was that many *pativratas* started ending their lives on the funeral pyre of the husband in the hope that they would thus be able to secure the company of their husband in the after life. It soon became a custom.

We hear of cases of the widow being forcibly buried along with the husband in the ancient times in countries like, Greece, Egypt, China and Japan. In Indian *sati* custom, the widow did the act of her free will. It was this ideal that led to even *sati* worship in later years.

The *Rigveda* makes no mention of the *sati* custom, but the *Atharvaveda* does give some hint. The *Shankha* and *Hariti Smritis* have high praise for the *sati,* but the *Manusmriti* and the *Yajnavalkya Smriti,* which have a greater following, do not mention this. They have prescribed that "the widow should lead a life of piety, without even thinking of another man."[2] It is remarkable to note that in our entire cultural history there is no evidence that a widow was ever forced to become a *sati*, which establishes that a widow became a *sati* out of her own free will.

A *pativrata*, if widowed, considered her duty to nourish her children. The Mahabharata says that on the death of Pandu, whereas Madri became a *sati*, Kunti felt it her duty to live to bring up her children. *Sati* was, however, at no stage considered to be an essential adjunct of *pativratya*. None of the queens of Dasharatha became *satis*, even though their children were grown up. Thousands of queens of Krishna, Satyavati (widow of Shantanu), Ambika and Ambalika (widows of Vichitravirya), widows of Kauravas,—none became *satis*.

Sati custom, however, continued to some extent. Alexander was surprised to see a large number of widows of warriors killed in battle performing *sati* in a group by the banks of the Sindhu. This would probably be the earliest example of the *jauhar* of the Rajput times. A Greek historian writes of an Indian commander in the Greek army, on whose death in the battlefield, each of his two widows fought for being allowed to become a *sati*.[3] The Greek historians have confirmed that the Indian widows performed, the *sati* voluntarily.[4]

Opposition to the system seems to have started in the 7th century AD. Bana (7th. century AD) says in the Kadambari that "*sati* can not prevent the husband from going to hell, she can not bring him back from there, she can not unite with him in the after life; rather she goes to hell like any person committing suicide." In the same period we know of Harshavardhana preventing his sister, Rajyashri, from becoming a *sati*. Later, in the 9th century AD the famous commentator, Medhatithi, declared *sati* to be anti-vedic and sinful like suicide.

The heroic act of *jauhar* by the Rajput women deserves a special mention in this context, being unparalleled in world history. The *jauhar* was performed by the Rajput women to escape falling into the hands of the Muslim conquerers on the death of their husbands in the battlefield. The case of performance of *sati* (*Jauhar*) by queen Padmini of Mewar along with thousands of women is well known. The second big *jauhar* was performed in Mewar itself in 1535AD by Rani Karnawati along with 13000 women.

In the days of India's decline the *sati* custom, which had originated with lofty ideals, deteriorated into an evil. The widows were, by and large, no longer guided by the desire to become one with the husband in the after life, but by the premonition of a miserable life ahead. Further, the relations of the widow, in order to usurp the property acquired by her in succession, forced her to the funeral pyre. When the evil reached its nadir, the rulers had to intervene. Akbar made efforts in this direction with partial success. The efforts of the Peshawas and Ahalyabai Holkar towards this end were also commendable. The Sikh *gurus*, specially Amaradasa, squarely denounced the custom. But all these efforts had only limited results.

The credit for finally putting an end to the *sati* goes to Lord William Bentick, the Governor-General of the East India Company. He made his conviction known through a Memorandum dated 8th Nov. 1829. There was some opposition by the traditionalists in the society. But Dwarakanath Tagore (grand father of Poet Rabindranath Tagore) and the most prominent social reformer, Raja Ram Mohan Roy, gave a forceful petition to the Governor-General to go ahead with his plans. The result was enactment of Prevention of *Sati* on 4th Dec. 1829, making *sati* a criminal offence. The traditionalists appealed to the Privy Council in London against it. Raja Ram Mohan Roy argued at the Privy Council in support of the Act, and the same was held valid.

The Act had a salutary effect in the British India. But it took time to take roots in the Indian states, because the British government did not want to interfere in their internal matters and cases of *sati* continued in Rajputana till 1861

AD. In the independent India we do hear stray cases of *sati*. But considering the vastness of the country and the antiquity of the custom, we can safely conclude that *sati* has ended and is no longer a social problem. However, *sati* memorials are held in high esteem and *satis* are worshipped, too, but it is only a recognition of the high ideals of this ancient custom.

References

1. Val. Ram. Ayodhya Kanda, 29. 17-18.
2. Manusmiti., 5.157.
   Yajngavalkya Smriti, Achara chapter 87.75.
3. C.V.Vaidya: Mahabharata sMimamsa, Translated by Madhav Rao Sapre.
4. *Ibid.*

12

The Role of the Woman in the Family, Social and Economic Provisions, *Stree Dhana* and Succession

In India ensuring cordial relationships in the family is a major test of a woman's intelligence, efficiency, circumspection and ability to manage in diversity. The Hindu woman generally enters an unknown family in an unknown environment, where she takes time to make her nature and feelings known to the members of the family and herself appreciate their problems and sensibilities. If this new entrant and the rest of the family are appreciative of one another, there is peace and harmony in the family, otherwise it disintegrates. We shall examine the status of woman's self respect against this background.

The oldest directive regarding woman's relationship with the family appears in the Rigveda[1]. That her self respect was given due importance is borne by the *mantra* blessings given to the bride at the time of marriage thus— '......You become the queen among the father-in -law, mother- in - law, sisters-in- law and younger brothers of the husband. It is probably this tradition that is behind calling the daughter-in-law '*Bahurani*'. Another honourable name, like '*bahurani*', is '*grihini*'. There is a code of conduct for the woman that earns her this exalted position. Kalidasa, in his drama *Shakuntalam* has beautifully described how the bride should conduct herself in the new family. *Rishi* Kanva, while bidding farewell to his adopted daughter, Shakuntala, had exhorted her to attain the position of *grihini* and to establish an atmosphere of peace and happiness in the new family.[2] Similarly the message of the *rishi* for Dushyanta had highlighted the need for respectful behavior of the husband towards the bride for the well being of the family, by calling her '*murtimati satkriya*' (embodiment of good conduct).[3]

The exhortation of *rishi* Kanva to the bride, contained in the words of Kalidasa, to conduct herself in an exemplary fashion towards the new family members is hallmark of Indian culture. Similar feelings have been echoed by Goswami Tulasidasa in his *Ramacharitra Manasa* through king Dasharatha. He called his queens and printed to them the secrets of ideal behaviour towards daughters-in-law.

The *Manusmriti* emphasizes the need for respect of the family towards the women for realizing worldly and spiritual goals. It says, "The family, where women feel miserable, gets destroyed soon. Where they are happy, it prospers. Gods dwell in families where women are respected, and where they are insulted, the religious rites performed by the family members go waste."[4] It is well known that women are fond of decorating themselves with fine dresses and ornaments on special occasions. To deprive them of these is very often at the root of family dissensions. Keeping this in view, the Manusmriti lays down, "Those desirous of worldly happiness must always provide their women with nice apparel, ornaments and eatables, specially on joyous occasions."[5]

The Indian family is the focal point in the national structure and all its members are constantly faced with opportunities for following high ideals. A nation is successful if its citizens work in unison for the common good. Similarly, the success of a family lies in its members exhibiting qualities of patience, sacrifice and willingness to be a leader in solving the problems facing the family. While the mother is an epitome of affection and sacrifice for her children, they, in turn, have the highest respect in the world for her. The husband tries to make the wife happy in every way, and the wife respects him like a god. The mother-in-law is served by the daughter-in-law and, she, in turn, gives her the same affection as to her own children.

Not in the least, it is considered essential to respect age and position of women. This is why the *Manusmriti*, while placing the mother above the father and the *acharya*, also instructs 'that the elder brother's wife, mother's sister, mother-in-law and father's sister should be respected like the *guru's* wife. The father's sister, mother's sister and elder sister must be respected like mother.'[6] Some examples are cited below.

The unparalleled example of respect towards elder brother's wife is that of Lakshmana towards Sita. Tulasidasa describes that in the forest, while walking behind Rama and Sita, Lakshmana used to ensure that his feet did not fall on their footsteps. This feeling is most poignantly described by Valmiki. When Rama asked Lakshmana to identify the ornaments of Sita collected by Sugriva when earlier dropped by her from high up, Lakshmana said, "I do not recognize the *keyuras* (arm bands) *kundalas* (ear rings), I know the *nupuras* (ornaments worn in the ankle) as I used to look at these alone while touching her feet daily."[7]

The *Mahabharata* describes an incident which brings forth the high ideals in the family. Once there was a severe famine in Kurukshetra. A Brahmana used to support the entire family by labouriously picking up fallen grains left over in the harvested fields after birds and poor people had also picked up. Now this, too, became scarce and the entire family started starving. One day the Brahmana procured some barley flour. While they were going to eat the same, a guest appeared. The Brahmana, not caring for his own life, offered his portion to the guest, which the latter finished in no time. Finding that the guest was still hungry, the wife presented her portion before the husband for giving away to the guest. But the Brahmana told her, "Even worms, animals and birds feed their females and protect their lives. By not protecting your life, I shall not only get a bad name in this world, but shall also go to hell. The wife is instrumental in acquisition of *dharma, kama, artha* by the husband and the service received from her is unparalleled. She bears a son, which enables the man to pay back the '*pitri rina*'."[8] This statement clearly outlines the duties of the husband towards the wife.

The reply of the Brahmani is illustrative of the high ideals of Indian womanhood. She said, "Mine and your *dharmas* are not separate. The highest god for a woman is her husband. It is only through him that she gets a son. Nobody on earth can give her greater blessing."[9] Unable to counter her argument, the man gave away the wife's portion to the guest.

As the guest was still hungry, the son also gave away his portion, saying that he must be a party to the performance of duty by the father. The guest was actually testing the Brahmana. He feigned as if he was still hungry. Not to be outdone, the daughter-in-law also gave up her portion. But the Brahmana refused, saying that he would not fulfill his duty towards a hungry guest that way. The daughter-in-law, however, argued, "I have learnt in childhood that just as there is *trivarga* (a group of three) in *garhasthya dharma* (duties of a house-holder); viz., *artha, kama* and *dharma*, there is a *trivarga* of son, grandson and *svarga* (heaven). The *dharma* of the son is to protect his forefathers from *naraka* (hell). The sons and the grandsons take them to the higher *lokas* (worlds)".[10] What she meant was that she had the same duty as her husband. Impressed by the logic, the Brahmana presented her portion as well to the guest. The guest was fully satisfied. The *Mahabharata* ranks this sacrifice equal to, if not greater than the '*Rajasuya yajna*' of Yudhishthira, being performed concurrently.

We also have the example of the Brahmana family of Ekachakra in the *Mahabharata,* mentioned earlier, in which each member vied with another in offering to go to the demon as his meal.

The contribution of women in maintaining family unity can also be gleaned from the exhortation of Sumitra in the *Valmikiya Ramayana* to Lakshmana—"Know Rama as your father and Sita as your mother and the forest as Ayodhya."[11] The advice of *rishi* Kanva to women, contained in his words—"Treat the co-wife as your dear friend,"—is exemplified in the extremely cordial relation between Subhadra and Draupadi, the two wives of Arjuna. Draupadi, Subhadra and other daughters-in-law were very reverent to Gandhari in spite of the fact that the Pandavas continued to suffer at the hands of Kauravas. Draupadi was unique in the service of her mother-in-law, Kunti. Kunti, on her part, loved her better than her sons. She had once expressed herself before Krishna thus—"Draupadi is an embodiment of all good qualities. She is dearer to me than my sons."[12]

Similarly, *Ramacharita Manasa* is very graphic in describing the love of Kaushalya for her daughter-in-law, Sita. Kalidasa depicts the ideal relationship in Raghuvamsha thus. On Rama's return from exile, Sita bowing before Kaushalya and Sumitra says, "I am very unfortunate as my husband had to undergo untold hardship on my account."[13] To this they reply, 'No, you are very auspicious. The safe return of Rama and Lakshmana is surely the result of your good deeds."[14] The poet, in a way, has pointed towards the duty of an ideal, mother-in-law who should try to alleviate the agony of the daughter-in-law by praising her qualities instead of holding her responsible for bad times for the family.

An incident in the *Mahabharata* is illustrative of the behavior of master of the house and other male members in the family towards the women in the family. When Sanjaya had met Yudhishthira at Upaplavya on the eve of the *Mahabharata* war as a messenger of Dhritarashtra, the latter, even though engrossed in serious political discussion with him, took special care to convey his concern and regard for the womenfolk in the family at Hastinapura. He wanted his love and regard to be conveyed to them. He also cautioned that they must not deviate from the ideals set for each family member.[15]

The wife's role has not been limited to participation in religious rites alone. She has been the kingpin around which the financial stability of the family revolves. An intelligent and contented housewife has been behind the prosperity of the family.

Cottage industries, including the use of the spinning wheel, had been receiving active participation of women from the Vedic times. In our own times Mahatma Gandhi had laid deep stress on the use of hand spun and hand woven khadi. He was convinced that this was a sure way towards economic self sufficiency. The *Vedas* are replete with artistic similes connected with spinning and weaving by the women. The *Rigveda* says, "The simple women, along with rearing their issues, carry on spinning and weaving at home like poets weaving thoughts..."[16] The *Yajurveda* says—thus while worshipping Indra with milk and *havana* the women are spinning fine yarn.[17] The *Rigveda* further says— "The Poets are watching the fine yarn spun by the two sisters and stretching the same between the sky and the ocean."[18] Further, "the mother is weaving intellect and clothes for her son."[19] The *Atharvaveda*, too, says, "Let the clothes woven by our wives, having fine texture and edges etc., be blissful for us."[20] In the same context, the *Yajurveda* says, "The two great women, Ushas and Ratri (dawn and night), are weaving colourful clothes and worshipping Indra."[21] A *mantra* in the *Atharvaveda* hints at association of several men and women in the process of weaving. In the Vedic period spinning and weaving of yarn for production of clothes was an important economic activity. The *Yajurveda* says,[22] "Let the yarn, giver of prosperity, add to the wealth."[23]

The above illustrations establish that women by themselves or in association with men were experts in the art of spinning and weaving of colouirful dresses and that it was a solid help towards the family economy. The Brahmanas, too, point to this. The Shatapatha Brahmana says that the spinning and weaving work of cotton and woollen cloth was that of women.[24]

It appears this cottage industry continued in later ages. Kautilya (4th century BC) mentions in his *Arthashastra* that the state had opened a weaving department which sent cotton to the blind and invalid women and widows and collected yarn through assistants, who were also women.[25] The Pali literature mentions an incident in which the wife was consoling her husband lying on death bed that he need not worry about the future of the family, as she was an expert in spinning and weaving.[26] The commentary of Medhatithi (9th century) on Manusmriti clarifies that a widow without a child and without adequate means of livelihood was to support the family through spinning and weaving.[27] This would indicate that this system was in vogue at least till 9th century A.D.

There is ample evidence that in the Vedic age fine cotton, woollen and silken dresses used to be woven. In due course this art developed into a flourishing trade with

Java, Sumatra and Bali etc. in the East and with the Roman empire in the West. In fact, it continued till the advent of the East India Company. The British market was flooded with fine garments from India, affecting the local industry badly. So the Company rulers went to the extent of cutting the thumbs of expert weavers of Bengal so as to put a stop to this trade. Worse still, it made our country dependent on the mills of Lancaster and Manchester for fine cloth. We have earlier mentioned how Mahatma Gandhi re-established this cottage industry. He was not satisfied with the indigenous production of cloth; he insisted on the use of khadi by everybody, more so by Congressmen. He had linked khadi with not only the freedom movement, but he was fully convinced of its economic viability. He saw in this a means of livelihood for the poor and the unemployed and economic emancipation of women. Even today *charkha* is a source of support for many helpless women. With fast industrialization, however, its future is sealed, unless Indian women take to it in a big way.

Streedhana and Succession

In Vedic times there was no distinction between men and women in matters of property, at least between the husband and the wife. Apastamba says, "The husband and the wife should perform religious rites jointly and both should have right over the family property. The wife is authorized to give alms out of it in absence of the husband." We do not know of any other civilization in which women had similar rights.

However, it is not clear whether the wife could succeed to the husband's property on his death. The view of Kane that in very old times the wife did not succeed to the husband's property, seems to be correct. For this he quotes Shakuntalam wherein the widow of an issueless merchant did not inherit the property.[28] It appears that even though

Gautama has admitted inheritance of the property of an issueless person by his widow, [29] Apastamba, Manu and Narada and even Kautilya do not do so. So this situation continued for a long time till the establishment of *Yajnavalkya Smriti* in the society.

Dayabhaga and *Mitakshara*

Even though the rights of women in the post-vedic era for Vedic studies became narrower, their right to property went up. The two main pillars of Property Laws for the Hindus; *Dayabhaga* of Jimutavahana and *Mitakshara* of Vijnaneshwar contributed to this change. Yajnavalkya *Smriti* on which *Mitakshara* is based, is liberal towards women's rights to property. *Dayabhaga* has been followed in Bengal and *Mitakshara* in rest of the country all along and these, with certain constitutional modification, are valid even today.

According to the Mitakshara, the sons and grandsons have a share in father's ancestral property by virtue of birth and none of the womenfolk could succeed to the same. But in *Dayabhaga* the son does not have an automatic right to the ancestral property, nor could the son claim division of the property during the lifetime of the father or grandfather. In the event of the death of the father or his becoming a recluse or *patita* (depraved) the children could claim division of the property. According to *Dayabhaga*, the widow inherits the husband's property, even if it is a joint one with brothers. According to *Mitakshara*, though the widow is not entitled to the joint property of the husband, she can inherit his property, if he dies issueless. Further, the deceased's father, brother etc. get his property only if wife, daughter, mother, or grandmother are not there. The only exception is the daughter's son, who also ranks only after wife and daughter. The *Dayabhaga* does not recognize women other than the widow, daughter, mother and grandmother etc. for succession.

Streedhana

According to the above laws the woman does not have unlimited right to the property acquired through succession. She can use it only for her living; she can not sell or squander it away. She could, however, mortgage it for specified purposes or sell it or partially donate it for the same. But the Hindu woman has a sole right to a type of property, defined by *shastras* as *streedhana*; and it is irrespective of the fact whether she belongs to a divided or undivided family. Nobody, not even the husband, has any legal right to interfere with this.[30] The laws of succession for this *streedhana* are also different, preference being given to women successors. The various *Smritis*, commentators and *Mitakshara*, however, differ amongst themselves as to what constitutes *streedhana*. But there is agreement that the first succession of *streedhana* goes to a woman. This is definitely an improvement in the property rights of women from the Mauryan times, because Kautilya had prescribed equal succession in *streedhana* for the son and the daughter.[31] Apastamba says that women's right to property, just like men's, is a very old custom. But there is no clear evidence that the wife was treated as successor to the property. Rather, a *mantra* in the *Rigveda*—'*na jamaye tanvo rikthamaraika*'[32] shows that only the son succeeded to the father's property and the daughter could not have it till the son was alive.

Ultimately it was laid down in the *Mitakshara* that the first successor to a man's property, if he dies without a son, is his widow. The main protagonists of this view are *Katyayana*, *Vishnu* and *Yajnavalkya Smritis*. In this case, next to the widow, the successors are daughter, mother, grandmother etc. and only in their absence, father, brother etc. According to the *Rigveda* the son got the entire succession, but *Manusmriti* prescribes that all the brothers must set apart a fourth of their portion for marriage of the sisters.[33]

A look at the ongoing liberation of property rights for women could indicate that our law makers were not at all rigid. The contrast elsewhere is revealing. According to the English Law, prior to the Act passed in 1882, the mere fact of marriage vested a right in the husband to the properties of the wife acquired by her from the mother's side, to that received by her at the time of marriage or there after, and also in all her personal moveable property.[34]

References

1. Rigveda, 10, 85.46.
2. Shakuntala, 4.18.
3. *Ibid.*, 5.16.
4. Manusmiti., 3-57-58.
5. *Ibid.*, 3.59.
6. *Ibid.*, 2.131-133.
7. Val. Ram., Kishkindha Kanda, 6.22-23.
8. Mahabharata, Ashvamedhic Parva.
9. *Ibid.*
10. *Ibid.*, 90.70-71.
11. Val. Ram., Ayodhya Kanda, 40.10.
12. Mahabharata,Udyoga Parva, 90.43.
13. Raghuvamsha, 14.5.
14. *Ibid.*,14.6.
15. Mahabharata, Udyoga Parva, 30.32.37.
16. Rigveda, 10.5.3.
17. Yaju.,20.43.
18. Rigveda, 1.159.4.
19. Rigveda, 5.47.6.
20. Atharvaveda., 14.2.51.
21. Yaju., 20.41.
22. Atharvaveda., 10.7.42.43.
23. Rigveda, 10.71.9; Yaju., 15.7.
24. Shat. Br.12.7.2.11.

25. Kautilya Arth., 2.23.
26. Manusmiti., 5.157; Medhatithi.
27. Ap. Dh. Su., 2.6.13.17-19.
28. P.V. Kane: History of Dharmashastra, Vol.ii, pt. I, p. 582.
29. Gautama dh. Su.
30. Yajna., 2.147.
31. Arth., 3.2.
32. Rigveda, 3.31.2.
33. Manusmiti., 9.118.
34. Married Women's Property Act 1882.

13
The Woman in Hindu Polity

The Indian woman has been given the pride of place in the society as the mistress of the household and her field of activity has been the house, the motherhood being deemed to be the fountainhead of the prosperity of the individual, society and the nation. But whenever need arose, she took up the reins of administration of the country in her hands and even led the nation's army. In this connection we would like to refer to the earliest vedic institutions, known as the *samiti, sabha* or *vidatha.,* The *samitis* and the *sabhas* were national institutions, the former being a sort of fore-runner of the present day Lok Sabha. The *sabha* was a cluster of regional bodies confined to villages, dealing with local and political issues and administering justice. Debates and recreation also fell within its purview. *Yajnas* were performed through it at the end of which discussion was held regarding their form and content. It was customary to narrate ancient lores, Narashansi etc. and give speeches, traditionally known as *vidatha.* The *Maitrayani Samhita* says— 'that is why only men go to the *vidatha,* not women.'[1] But the evidence in the *Rigveda* should be taken as authoritative, wherein the bridegroom exhorts his bride at the time of marriage—'May you speak at the *vidatha* with authourity.'[2] Furthermore, the *Tattiriya Samhita* talks of an exclusive organization of women for discussing their problems, rights and responsibilities.[3] The *Chhandogya Upanishad,* too, mentions spiritual conferences in those days at which women also participated, as seen from examples of Gargi and Sulabha.

The Buddhist literature mentions of religious voyages by Sanghamitra and other nuns. We also know of the debate between Mandana Mishra and Shankaracharya at which Ubbaya Bharati had presided. Thus, we find participation by women in *sabhas* even in later days, though it seems to have been restricted in the *Mahabharata* time. A case in point is assertion of Draupadi at the kingly court that the Kauravas had sullied *sanatana dharma* by dragging her to the *sabha*.

We find evidence of women taking part in politics and even running the administration in very ancient times. Kalidasa has described how on the death of Agnivarna, his widow who was pregnant at that time and with no other issue, had taken up the reins of the kingdom in her hands.[4] The name of Vidula ranks very high amongst the great women well versed in politics and administration. In an earlier context, we have narrated how she had exhorted her son to fight the enemy and get back his kingdom. We have also seen how Kunti had reminded Yudhishthira to fight for his rights, uttering the famous words—"Do not have any misgivings as to whether circumstances make the king or the king frames the same; verily the king is the creator of *kala* (circumstances).[5] How true it is that the well being of the nation lies in the hands of the king or those who are running the government, be it a democracy, dictatorship or a socialist regime! Satyavati also tendered advice to Bhishma regularly in running the kingdom. Instances of Draupadi giving sound political advice to the Pandavas are also found.

The cave engravings at Nanaghat depicting Queen Nayanika along with the king, Shatakarni, (2nd century BC) are a pointer to this trend. She had governed the state on behalf of her minor children, Vedashri and Shaktishri.

Similarly, Prabhavati Gupta (4th century AD) of Wakataka dynasty, Vijaya Bhattarika (7^{th}century AD) of Chalukya dynasty, Sugandha and Didda of Kashmir (10th century AD) administered huge kingdoms on behalf of their minor sons. Jayamati ruled over Kashmir after the death of her husband. An example in the 4th century AD is that of Queen Kumaradevi whose picture is found engraved on the coins of Chandragupta.[6] Harshacharita indicates active co-operation of the sister, Rajyashri, to Harshavardhana in administrative matters. Further, appointment of women to important posts of Rajyapala was a common feature of the Chalukyan rule in the 10th-11th century AD.[7] Minaldevi, mother of the powerful ruler, Siddharaja Jayasimha, had ruled over Gujrat in the 11th century AD. Much later, Queen Durgavati of Jodhpur had defended the kingdom in a valiant fight against Aurangzeb. Ranis Ahalyabai and Lakshmibai had upheld the tradition. Vajpai, giving experts from *Niti Prakasha* (ch, 2, sh. 45-47) has established that women used to receive training in the use of arms alongwith political training in Vedic times.[8] The *Rigveda*[9] mentions that 'Vishpala, wife of Khela, had fought the enemies and won a thousand cows, also mentions of formation of a women's wing in the army of Dasa Namucha. Danu, mother of Vritrasura had gone to the battlefield with her son. Kaikeyi had accompanied Dasharatha to the *devasura* war and had rendered valuable help.

Sanskrit dramas indicate that women, expert in archery, used to be appointed body guards to the kings. The women of Karnataka were famous for defending their homes. Records show that a woman warrior of Mysore had died fighting in a village against intruders in 1041 AD and that another one had been awarded for arresting dacoits in 1264 AD. The Nilagunda edict mentions one Mandaleshvari as head of an army. A woman warrior of Shimoga Taluka died in 1446 AD fighting the enemies.[10]

The dexterity of Rajput women in warfare, military manoevres and administration is well known. They preferred that their husbands and sons died fighting in the battlefield in the best traditions of the Kshatriyas, rather than running back defeated. It is a historical fact that the Queen of Jodhpur had got the gates of the fort closed upon Maharaja Yashawant Singh, when he had turned back fighting against Aurangzeb. The valour of Rani Karnavati is well known, who on the death of her husband, Samarasi, had trounced Qutubuddin. Rani Jawaharbai, widow of Rana Sanga, had herself led the army against Bahadur Shah and died valiantly. Rani Durgavati of Gondwana is still remembered for giving up her life fighting against the mighty army of Akbar.

A Holkar Rani, Bhimadevi, had told Sir John Malcolm that even Maratha princesses used to be trained in warfare. The kingdom of Kolhapur was founded by a woman. Kamalabai Sindhia is known for her military acumen. The names of Jijabai, Umabai etc. are equally well known in Maratha history. So does the name of Rani Lakshmibai of Jhansi stand out in recent times.

References

1. Maitrayani Samhita, 4.7.1.
2. Rigveda, 10.85.26.
3. Cultural Forum, Jan.1964 p.123.
4. Raghuvamsha of Kalidasa, sarga 19.
5. Mahabharata, Udyoga Parva, 132.17.
6. Allen: Gupta coins.
7. R.K. Mukherji: The Gupta Empire, p. 46.
8. Ambika Prasad Vajpai: Hindu Rajyashastra p. 286.
9. Rigveda, 1.112.10; 118.8.
10. A.S. Altekar: Position of Women in Hindu Civilization.

14
Woman in Indian Art

Shilpa (art) has been considered a major constituent of skills since earliest times. There is a mention in the *Chhandogya Upanishad* how Narada in the list of the '*devajnana*' *vidyas* mastered by him has enumerated *shilpa* as well.[1] The *Shukranitishastra* metions 32 vidyas and 64 skills, including Art. The Jain texts enumerate 72 skills, including *vatthu vijja* (architecture). The term '*shilpa*' has been mostly taken to cover architecture, sculpture and painting.

According to Coomaraswamy, the noted art critic, the 'early Aryans were experts in handicrafts, architecture, goldsmithy, making of wooden chariots and metal utensils needed for daily use and in *yajnas*, etc'. They knew spinning and weaving, leather work, and making of clay pottery. Though there is no evidence of statues, the artefacts made by them were certainly artistic. It is quite likely that initially art was confined to decoration alone.'[2] The excavations at Mohenjodaro pertaining to Indus Valley Civilization (3000 BC-2500 BC) throw light on existence of Art at that time.[3] Sir William Orpan states that "so far there is no evidence of Art in the Bronze age, unless we ignore the seals and armour with animal figurines cast in them similar to the feminine form terracotta depicting ornaments worn by women in those days."[4] He himself explains the logic for non-availability of substantial evidence thus—"Though India had excelled in literature and architecture, there are very few signs of sculpture and painting. Most of these have been lost, because these were not preserved the way it was done in Mesopotammia and Egypt. As a matter of fact, Indian Art found expression in Buddhist Art first, though their wooden carvings depicting gods and goddesses smack of the Hindu pantheon."[5] It stands to reason that these arte facts perished due to lack of preservation. Because, "we do know from Brahmana texts that many types of *vedis* (sacrificial altars) and *chitis* (decorative engravings for the altars) used to be prepared, which subsequently gave birth to the science of geometry.[6] In fact, from certain ***Vedic mantras*** and from the Sanskrit manuscript '*Yantra Sarvasva*' found at Vadodara we see that even certain types of planes were constructed in the vedic age.[7] We shall, however, not go into this question, being beyond our scope.

The excavations at Harappa of Indus Valley Civilization have brought to light ivory seals, terracotta statues of mother goddess, gold ornaments, coins, clay vessels and remains of multi-storeyed baked brick buildings. The limestone statuettes, terracotta and metal statues, and human figurines on seals go to establish that the artists of that time were conversant with various art media and modes. The two famous statuettes, of red and blue stone each found at Harappa are examples of exquisite art. Similarly, the copper statue of a dancing girl found at Mohenjodaro is unique in itself. When we compare these ancient pieces of art with those in the historical period, we are amazed at the similarities, in spite of a gap of nearly two thousand years and are led to conclude that the art traditions established in those pristine days continued, some even till today.[8]

This continuity in art traditions spread over the entire country in varying degrees and forms reminds us of the cultural unity of India[9]. Dr. V.S. Agarwal writes[10]—"The terracotta plaque found at Ahichhatra depicts a cloth roll, which is the same as included in the gifts sent by King Bhaskaravarmana of Kannauj to King Harsha as mentioned by Bana. Bana describes how the pearl necklace, named Mandakini, gifted to the great King Satavahana by Nagarjuna, had, in due course found its way to King Harsha. This shows that valuable artifacts used to circulate throughout the country.

Though in India sublime art has been based on religion and spirituality, the temporal aspect has not been lost sight of. Bharata Aiyer says—"The preponderance in all ages of female statues depicting varieties of female beauty does not match with the thinking that Indian Art was confined to religious and spiritual themes."[11] Against this background, we shall go into depiction of women in art in some detail.

A nude female figure carved on a gold leaf, said to be of Mother Goddess belonging to 8th or 9th century BC is indicative of deployment of artistic statues in religious practice. [12] The Ardhanarishwara images of Mahadeva and Parvati, each in half, symbolizing the Paramatma (Almighty) and Shakti (Primordial Power), in a way, highlight the basic unity of man and woman. Similarly, the statues of Radha and Krishna on the one hand, and Krishna and gopis on the other, denote the unity of the *jivatma* with the Paramatma.

Probably the oldest depiction of woman is the bronze statue belonging to the Indus Valley Civilization. The depiction of woman in the form of a *yakshini* is, however, very common. The *yakshini* images of the Mauryan (4th-3rd century BC) and the Shunga period (2nd century BC) and those found at the Kankali Tila are unique in the artistic depiction of women. Further, depiction of women in the terracotta of Mauryan and Shunga periods would go to establish that women had an important place in the society at large. A statue found at Amaravati depicts women worshipping the lotus and the footprints symbolic of the Buddha's birth. The famous *torana* at Sanchi (2nd-1st century BC) shows two elephants offering water with their trunks on Mayadevi, mother of the Buddha.

The Bhita plaque of the Shunga period depicts a scene from the drama Shakuntala. A statue of Mayadevi found at Shoharatgarh in Siddartha Nagar district of U.P., depicting the birth of the Buddha, is a fine example of an artistic representation of the story in the Buddhist literature. The clay statues of heavily ornamented women pertaining to the Shunga period, found at the ancient site of Siswania in Basti district of U.P. throw light on the dresses of women in those days. The Karali devi image of the Rajput times throws light on Shakti worship. The craze for ornaments amongst women in the Shunga period is evident from the statue of Prithvidevi. While on the subject a reference is also invited to a plaque depicting a beautiful, heavily ornamented female figure found by Durgavati Tripathi at the afore-mentioned Siswania, which she had gifted to the State Archaeological Museum at Lucknow. Page 40 of 'The Report on working and progress of the museums of U.P., 1950' makes a special mention of this exquisite piece of art of the Shunga period. Chandra Chur Mani had found an exquisite female statuette belonging to the Mauryan period at Siswania. At other sites Durgavati Tripathi had found an ancient and rare, though undated, statue of Parvati in the centre flanked by Ganesha and Kartikeya and another one of Varahi devi. These point to different modes of worship current in the specific periods.[13]

The Buddhist *chaitya* at Karla in Maharashtra carved out of rocks in the Shunga period (1st century AD) is an exquisite example of Indian architecture. One of the statues here depicts a man alongwih his wife, giving *dana* (charities) highlighting the close association of the wife in religious rites. Similarly, existence of both men and women side by side in a procession depicted in statues preserved at Mathura museum throws light on the position of women in the contemporary society. The female images in the Nageshvaraswamy temple at Kumbhakonam, constructed in the 10th century AD, provide similar evidence. The contribution of Kumara devi, Queen of Govindachandra of Kannauj (1144A.D.), to the growth of architecture in her time is well known. She had constructed many Buddhist *viharas* at Shravasti and Sarnath. The Dharmachakra Jina vihara at Sarnath constructed by her, with a grand statue of the Buddha in the centre and with fine sculpture is a milestone. The Mathura museum has an exquisite female head and the Kashi Hindu Vishvavidyalaya has a stone image showing the scene of churning of curd by the *gopis*. Both these are fine examples of depiction of women in art in the 6th century A.D. Sanchi and Amaravati *stupas* are unique in depiction of female beauty and motherhood. A 7 foot high statue of an ordinary woman in Besnagar (Gwalior district), said to be of 3rd century Mathura style, would go to show that even ordinary women had an honourable place in society.[14]

Starting from the Mohenjodaro age, various types of ornaments, headgear and hairstyles depicted in the female statues achieved a climax in the Gupta age. The female statues of Gupta age found in excavations at Ahichhatra and Rajghat (in Varanasi) are seen to be giving expression to the hairstyles described in literature as *chhatrakara* (umbrella shaped), *simantaka* (with borders), *bhramaraka* (bee-like), *madhumakshika* (honey-comb) etc. Depiction of dance styles is also found in sculpture, reaching excellence in examples like, the *tandava nritya* of Nataraja and *tribhanga mudra* of a woman. Women find a special expression in murals as well. The murals at Badami (6th centurt AD), Sittanavasala (7th centurty AD), Ellora and Kanchipuram (8th century AD), and at Tanjore are typical examples. The murals in the palaces of Malabar and Cochin in the 17th and 18^{lh} century AD respectively are simply fascinating. The Tanjore murals show a woman engrossed in cosmetics. The murals in the Brihadishvara temple at Tanjore are famous for depiction of queens.

A unique case of depiction of a woman in a coin is that of Kumara devi, Queen of Chandragupta I., which hints at participation of women even in statecraft.

Later, in the 15th century depiction of women was found to have started in the Rajput, Mughal and Jain styles of painting in manuscripts. The Jain manuscript '*Kalpa Sutra*'(c. 1439 A.D.) found at Mandu and now in the National Museum in Delhi depicts the birth of Tirthankara Arishtanemi in a painting therein. A number of Illuminated Manuscripts— Tibetan, Nepalese, Oriya and Gujrati etc.— exhibited in the Kala Bhavan of the B.H.U. contain female figures. The Rajput school of painting, apart from *bhakti* (devotion), excels in depiction of women's *shringara* (decoration) and their response to emotional situations like, separation from the beloved and the joy of reunion etc. This school is widely recognized for its excellent visualization of *ragas* and *nayika-bheda*. The paintings of Radha Krishna, Gopi Krishna and Nala Damayanti are some of the well known examples.

Sanskrit literature throws light on aptitude of women for painting. We find from *Shakuntalam* of Kalidasa and *Uttara Ramacharita* of Bhavabhuti that women of those days were lovers of painting. The Ratnavali of Harsha depicts the heroine, Sagarika, to be such an expert as to be able to make a painting of the King after seeing him only once. The treatises like, *Chitra Lakshana* and *Vishnu Dharmottara* etc. have discussed the technicalities of the art of painting. Vatsyayana, too, in his *Kama Sutra* has defined the *shadangas* (six constituents) of painting. The most exquisite examples of *shadanga chitrana* are found in the murals of Ajanta. One of the best pieces (6th century AD) is the depiction of Buddha standing as a monk with the begging bowl in the right hand, Yashodhara standing in front holding Rahula's hand in her left hand and with her right hand on Rahula's shoulder and directing him to ask for his patrimony from the father. One wonders at the multiplicity of emotions depicted in a single painting![15]

It is equally noteworthy that love of painting became a natural instinct with our women. The talent of even ordinary women in depicting rural scenes – animals, birds, wells, varieties of human forms, flowers and leaves etc. on the door jambs and walls and in *alpanas* (painting on the floor) can certainly not go unnoticed.

References

1. Chhan. Up., 7.1.2.
2. Anand K. Coomaraswamy: History of Indian and Indonesian Art, p. 8.
3. V.S.Agarwal: Indian Art, p. 18.
4. The Outline of Art: Ed. Sir William Orpen, p. 360 Revised by Horace Ship.
5. *Ibid.*
6. Ram Govind Dwivedi: Vaidic Sahitya, p. 148.
7. Ibid p. 361.
8. Bharat Aiyar; Indian Art: A short Introduction, p. 37.
9. *Ibid.*
10. V.S.Agarwal:Indian Art, p. 294.
11. Bharat Aiyar: Indian Art, A short Introduction.
12. Mulk Raj Anand: The Hindu View of Art, p. 18.
13. These statues belonged to the private collection of Smt. Durgavati Tripathi of Basti, U.P.
14. V.S.Agarwal: Studies in Indian Art, p.116, Vishvavidyalaya Prakashan, Varanasi.
15. Prof. N.N. Ghosh: Bharat ka Prachina Itihasa p. 4291 (Hindi Translation by Chandra Chur Mani, Indian Press, Allahabad, 1951).

15
Spiritual Attainment of Women

Women's participation in the *yajnas* has been a must from the early Vedic times. This right remained intact even after the study of the *Vedas* was forbidden later on for them. In *Vedic* times they were also encouraged to attain *moksha,* the highest goal for humans. We know the *Vedic rishis* had delved into the closest secrets of the universe and had propounded spiritual theories, the like of which has not been seen by the humanity in its ongoing journey of several millennia, the best example being the 'Nasadiya sukta'. Many of the profound *suktas* had been created by women *rishikas*—Vak, Ghosha (of the famous Devisukta), Apala, Lopamudra, Vishvavara, Sikata, Surya, Indrani, Sarparajni, Mamata, Yami, Romasha, Juhu, Nivavari, Urvashi, Shraddha, etc.

Many women had acquired high spiritual attainment in the Upanishadic period, too. That the path of *moksha* was not barred for women is also established from the fact that Kapila, originator of Sankhya, had taught this first to his mother, Devahuti.[1] The *Hariti Smriti* tells us of *brahmavadinis* and *Baudhayana Dharmasutra* even talks of taking to *sanyasa* by women, as per Mitakshra. But older still is the evidence of the Brihadaranyaka Upanishad, where Maitreyi has been addressed as *brahmavadini*. The same Upanishad also mentions Gargi, who had participated in the philosophical conference convened by Janaka. We find a reference in the *Mahabharata* of Sulabha of the

Upanishadic times, who was well versed in the Sankhya and *yoga*. So does Bhavabhuti vividly describe how Atreyi wandered from *ashrama* to *ashrama* in search of spiritual knowledge.[2] Kalidasa has mentioned about the recluse Kaushiki in *Malavikagnimitra* and Patanjali, regarding the nun, Shankara, which would go to indicate that taking to *sanyasa* was permitted in the Vedic religion to women in the Shunga period.

The *Mahabharata* mentions Satyavati going in for *tapasya*, Gandhari going with Dhritarashtra into *vanaprastha* and Kunti going in *sanyasa*. *Sanyasa*, however, came to be forbidden by the 6th century AD for women, so much so that the *Atri Smriti* even went on to brand *sanyasa* as the cause of downfall of women.[3] Apparently, slackening of moral behaviour must have been behind this stricture.

The fact that the Buddha was initially opposed to sanyasa for women shows that the above prohibition had gained ground in society (*Vinaya Pitaka, Chulla Vagga, Pajapati Pabajja Sutta*). But the Buddha subsequently, though reluctantly, permitted *pravajya* (*sanyasa*) to women for admission to the Bauddha *sangha* laying down very tough eight rules of conduct for them. He said, "I have established eight hard rules for the *bhikshunis* for observance throughout their life to ensure avoidance of immorality."[4] In spite of this he was fearful of the evil consequences of relaxation and prophesied that with women entering the Bauddha *sangha,* it would last only for five centuries as against ten otherwise. He, however, never differentiated between the *bhikshus* and *bhikshunis* in matters of religious teaching. Many women entered the Bauddha *sangha* in Buddha's lifetime itself, the first amongst them being Mahaprajapati Gautami, his mother's sister. Even Amrapali was accepted, which transformed her life.

Many *bhikshunis* not satisfied merely with their own spiritual attainment, went ahead to preach the new religion. Thus, Sanghamitra *theri,* daughter of Ashoka, was the first woman in the world to travel to a foreign country for spreading her religion. She had gone to Tamralipti (Sri Lanka), had converted the king's sister, Anuladevi, with a number of women to Buddhism and had established the *bhikshuni sangha.*

The *theris* have the same honoured position in Buddhism as *sthaviras* (*theras*), which is evident from the *Therigatha*—a composition of seventy *theris*. This is compendium of their spiritual practices. Buddha himself was impressed with the spiritual attainment of certain *theris*. We also find from *Etadaggavagga* that he had given the pride of place to many *theris* in matters of specialized knowledge and practices. Some of these were—Mahaprajapati Gautami among *bhikshuni-shravikas,* Khema, Queen of Bimbisara, among *mahaprajnas,* Utpalavarna among *ridhimatis,* Patachara among *vinayadharas,* Dhammadinna among *dharmakathikas,* Nanda among *dhyanis,* Bhadra Kundalakesha among *kshiprabhijnas,* Bhadra Kapilayini among *purvajanma-anusmritijnas,* Bhadra Katyayini, Rahula's mother, among *mahabhijnanapraptas,* Krisha Gautami among *ruksha-chivaradharinis,* Shrigalamata among *shraddhalus,* Sujata, daughter of Senani, among *upasika Shravikas,* Vishakha Mrigaramata, among the *dayikis,* Khujja Uttara among *bahushrutas,* Samavati, Queen of King Udayana of Vatsa, among *maitriviharapraptas,* Supravasa among *pranitadayikas,* Supriya among the servers of the sick and Grihapatni among *vishvasikas.*

In Jainism women had the right to *sanyasa* from the days of the originator of the religion, Parshvanatha himself (250 years before Mahavira). However, it was not permitted in the Digambara sect due to impracticability of remaining naked. Unlike Buddhism, the *sadhvi* enjoys lesser position than the *sadhu* in Jainism. Further, certain portions of the Mahaparijnana, Aninopatata, and Drishtivada are out of bounds for her. In the early days of Jainism women could become a recluse even during the lifetime of the husband and live in *mathas*. There are examples of many princesses and well to do women giving up worldly pleasures and taking to the austere life of a nun. The foremost comes the name of Piyadansa, the daughter of Mahavira (6th century B.C.) himself, who had renounced the world soon after embracing Jainism. The Jain texts give an account of Jayanti, daughter of King Sahasranika of Kaushambi, who had accepted Jainism after a profound discussion on spiritual matters with Mahavira and had soon renounced the world, Kumaradevi, of whom we have read in a previous chapter, led a wholly spiritual life. The rock edict excavated at Sarnath praises her religiosity in eloquent terms. Names of *bhikshunis* Gutta, Anopama, Sumedha etc. also find a special mention as preachers of Buddhism. According to Ghosh, this Kumaradevi was different from the Queen of Chandragupta I. She had dedicated her whole life to the spread of Buddhism and is considered next only to Mallika, Shyamavati, Sanghamitra, Charumati and Rajyashri in this regard. Her son, Vijayachandra (1155-1170 A.D.), had erected a grand *chaitya* at Kashi.[5]

Lord Krishna had opened the doors to spiritual quest for women by harmonizing *bhakti* (devotion to God) with *sankhya* and *karma yogas*. He clearly tells Arjuna—"Those who worship me selflessly, while performing their prescribed *karmas*, are of *satvic* (pure) nature, be they men or women."[6] Thus, *bhakti marga* provided equal scope to men and women. *Shrimad Bhagavata Purana* and similar texts were created with the *bhakti marga* propounded by Lord Krishna as the base. A vast tradition of *kathas, kirtanas, vratas* etc. was created in the wake of *bhakti marga*. These found special attraction for women. In the *bhakti marga* there was never any discrimination between men and women, high or low. It was against this background that Tulasidasa highlighted the anecdote of Shabari in the *Ramayana*.

Bhakti marga spread far and wide in India during the medieval period. It was nurtured by the *sakhis* and *banis* of Nirgunapanthi saints and poets and by the devotional poetry of the Sagunapanthis.The Sagunapanthi saints created a wave of hope amongst the downtrodden that even they could attain *moksha* by devotion to Rama and Krishna.

The Bhagavata *dharma* taught by Lord Krishna had taken deep roots not only amongst the Vrishnis, but had gained wide acceptance all over. Krishna considered the *artas* (utterly helpless ones) as the highest amongst the four types of *bhaktas*[7] and Draupadi was one such at the shameful hour of her attempted undressing at the court of Dhritarashtra. Bhakta Suradasa also describes very poignantly as to how the *gopis* had left Uddhava, who had come to dissuade them from the path of devotion and, instead, take to that of *jnana* and *yoga,* nonplussed. This underlines the general preference of women for the *bhakti marga.*[8]

There is a gallaxy of women saints in India. In the glorious tradition of saints in South India, Andala (born 773 A.D.) of the Alawara cult[9] had earned great fame for her *bhakti.* Her devotional songs appear in the famous Tamil book *Tiruppavai.* Similarly, Molla is famous for her Telugu *Ramayana.* The Krishna *bhakti* of Mirabai (1498-1573 A.D.) is well known.[10] Earlier, the Jhala Rani, said to be a Queen of Rana Sanga (1482-1527 A.D.) is said to have acquired the status of a saint herself on becoming a disciple of Sant Ravidasa. Much later we have the case of Sahajobai, a disciple of Sant Charana Dasa, who was not only a saint herself, but had written a book "*Sahajobai ki Bani—Sahaja rakasha*". Likewise, Suvachana Dasi (born 1671 A.D.) was a saint in the Udasi cult of the Sikhs, who had written several books like, *Prema Tarangini, Vijnana Sagara, Videha moksha,* etc.

The brief narrative above is adequate to establish that women were not far behind men in the spiritual field. It presents a big contrast with the belief in certain cultures that, let alone equality, women had no souls.

References

1. Bhagavata, 3.33.30.
2. See Chapter, pages.
3. Atri smriti, 136.137.
4. Rahula Sankrityayana: Buddhacharya, pp. 73-74.
5. Prof. N.N.Ghosh: Bharat ka Prachina Itihasa, Hindi Translation by C.C. Mani, Publisher, Indian Press, Allahabad.
6. Shrimadbhagavata., 11.25.10.
7. Gita, 7.16.
8. Surasagara.
9. Acharya Ram Chandra Shukla: Hindi Sahitya ka Itihasa, Sanshodhita Sanskarana, p. 192.
10. Parashuram Chaturvedi:Uttara Bharata ki Sant Parampara.

16

Impediments to Social Development: Dowry and Purdah Systems

Dowry (*Yautuka*)

Our Shastras have decried marriages in which *Kanya shulka* or bride price was taken by the father of the bride. Some *Smritis* did, no doubt, permit acceptance of one or two she-calves and one or two he-calves, from the bridegroom in the *arsha vivaha* but even this was considered by Manu as not in keeping with the spirit of *kanyadana*. He clearly says—"Some people consider taking a pair of cows from the bridegroom as valid under the Arsha *vivaha*, but it tantamounts to sale, irrespective of the amount being big or small."[2] Bhishma also corroborates the same idea in the *Mahabharata*.[3] The *Mahabharata* says—"a person who sells his son for money and one who takes bride-price for earning a living are both great thieves and go to hell."[4] Baudhayana went to the extent of laying down that "a bride who is married through *kanya shulka* loses her rights as a wife. She could only be treated as a slave."[5] Atri Smriti also says—"In a marriage with *kanya shulka* the bride is not to be treated as a wife, but as a slave and a son born out of such a marriage is not entitled to perform *pinda dana* (offerings to the ancestors).[6] The *Padma Purana* goes a step further by saying that "the wise should not even see the face of a seller of bride; if perchance he has done so, he must look at the sun at once."[7]

Due to the prohibition by the *Puranas* and *Dharmashastras* and in the light of example of high ups, *kanya shulka* came to be regarded as reprehensible. In the *Mahabharata* Arjuna, while vowing to kill Jayadratha, said that if he failed to do so, he would be committing, among other sins, sin of accepting *kanya shulka*.[8] Even then the custom did not die out. We find that when Bhishma proposed to Shalya, King of Madra, to marry his sister, Madri, to Pandu, the latter asked *kanya shulka* from him. He said that he was doing so in keeping with the family tradition.[9] Dr. Altekar mentions an edict of the 15th century AD at Tanjore through which the Brahmanas prescribed outcasting of acceptors of *kanya shulka*. This would indicate that the custom was in vogue at that time.[10] The custom is practically non-existent today and if someone due to poverty does so, he does it in a clandestine manner. The *Shrimad Bhagavata* mentions a fine example of *kanya shulka* in ancient India. *Rishi* Richika had requested king Gadhi for the hand of his daughter, Satyawati, in marriage and the latter had asked him for one thousand fine horses as *kanya shulka*. The *rishi* had to tkae the help of god Varuna to comply with this tough demand.

The dowry system, though a social evil was not so initially. It was considered honourable for the bride's father to offer dresses, vehicles, ornaments etc. to the bridegroom, all of which was called *yautuka*. The bridegroom's father and close relations were also given gifts. All this was done voluntarily and it was never a precondition to marriage. Side by side we also come across rare cases of refusal of *yautuka* like, the case of Sukanya, who had returned her father's ornaments etc. on reaching the cottage of her husband and changing into recluse's clothes. The Ramayana and the *Mahabharata* are replete with examples of *yautuka* amongst the high-ups. Even ordinary people are seen to be taking pride in pleasing the bride and the groom with gifts. Ghosh mentions that 'Bimbisara had married the daughter of the Koshala king, Mahakoshala, who had given a village of Kashi to him in dowry.'[11]

But the custom of *yautuka* became a cancer of society in later years. There is no doubt that disregard of ideals of marriage and child marriage lay at the root. By and by interest in *shastric* studies and *brahmacharya* waned, resulting in decrease in the marriageable age of the boys. Further, with the prohibition of Vedic studies and *brahmacharyashrama* for the girls tendency of marrying them off at an early age gained ground. So much so that even the *Smritis* started stressing that if the father did not marry off the girl before she started her menses, he invited the sin of abortion. This also resulted in fathers of girls tempting eligible boys with the lure of a good dowry. Many a father succumbed to the temptation and the boys themselves were too small to decide for themselves. The outcome was marriage between very young boys and girls. In course of time, the fathers of grooms stooped down to the level of settling a dowry in the shape of money, horses and elephants etc. Thus the curse of dowry replaced the voluntary offering of *yautuka*.

This cursed custom led to gradual decline of the Hindu society during the thousand years of Muslim rule. Cases started coming up where people did not consider anything wrong in cancelling a settled marriage, even after the *tilaka* ceremony, if a higher bid was at hand. What was needed was a new *Smriti* to prohibit this!

Families continued to get destroyed. It was only when in the beginning of the 19th century AD a girl named Snehlata of Bengal ended her life by burning, being unable to bear her father's worry regarding arranging her dowry that a serious movement was born against the dowry system. But the leaders of society lacked strong will and transparency. They would write articles and address gatherings, but when occasion of a young man's marriage in their own family arose, they never thought twice of accepting the dowry in a clandestine manner. This killed the movement itself. The society had already fallen from the high ideals of marriage. The demand for dowry soared. Not only the parents, but the boys themselves, even those with high education and reformist past, never felt ashamed in placing demands for dowry. A ray of hope, however, came with the country's independence. After prolonged efforts the Parliament passed Anti-dowry Act, 1961. According to this it is a cognizable offence to offer or to accept dowry, which means any property or money or valuable securities etc. either before or after or at the time of marriage. This, however, does not cover provisions in the 'shariat' or 'mehr' amongst the Muslims.

It is, however, to be realized that mere passing of the Act is not going to end this menace. The leaders of the society will have to wage a relentless war against it to prevent it from becoming ineffective, like the Sharda Act. The politicians, revelling in their preserve, could find a lot to do in this direction. The students, too, who are fond of going on a strike at the slightest pretext, could contribute a lot. A change in attitude towards marriage is also called for. It should not be the obligation of the bride's father alone to look for a suitable match. The boy's father should also feel an equal obligation to do so. This is not an entirely new concept. In the olden days even the *rishis* used to ask for a suitable wife to help them in proper performance of religious rites.

The Purdah System

The purdah system may have begun in a harmless fashion, but as the days went by it did become a curse for the society. The contact with the West and the efforts of reformers have, however, practically ended it. In the not too distant past men had to guard their purdah clad women like baggage at railway stations, in fairs and other crowded places. Cases were not uncommon when purdah clad brides got interchanged at crowded railway platforms and reached wrong destinations in a palanquin. Ignorance and lack of education made the situation worse. The women were forced to remain in purdah, thirsting for a glimpse of the outside world. It was a matter of great dishonour for the family if the bride so much as stepped outside the house without the purdah. No thought was given to the immense harm to her health.

The spread of education, coupled with the changing political and economic scene, proved to be effective in eradicating this evil. Most noteworthy was Gandhi's *andhi* (Tempest of Gandhi) which exhorted women to come out of purdah and participate in the struggle for freedom. Mention of one incident will suffice. In 1932 when *satyagraha* was at its peak and Mahatma Gandhi and other top leaders were in jail, many women came out of purdah and exhibited their might. There was no purdah in the unorthodox Nehru family, but it was very much there in the orthodox family of Madan Mohan Malaviya. While Sarup Rani Nehru with her daughters and daughters-in-law joined the struggle, even Kundan Devi of the Malaviya family came out of purdah and faced police lathis, thus setting an example for others.

While investigating the origin of the purdah system, we are amazed at the early days of *svayamvara*, when there was a total lack of this custom. But it should be remembered that decorum was maintained on all occasions. Kalidasa vividly describes how at the *svayamvara*, in spite of her ill-concealed attraction towards Aja, Indumati did not transgress decorum.[12] This is in utter contrast to the other extreme of shameless behaviour of some present day women blindly aping the West.

The purdah system was definitely non-existent in ancient times. Equally certain is the fact that it was synchronous with the arrival of Muslims in India. A tangible evidence is non-existence of this custom in the South where

Muslim influence has been nominal. The fact that this is being rigidly followed by the Muslims even now adds weight to the assertion.

Ghosh, while describing the status of Mauryan society says—"Women were free in all respects. They studied philosophy and could even become a recluse. It is the Muslims who started the purdah system."[13] Sanghamitra's travel to Simhala is a case in point. We also find Ajanta frescoes depicting women alongwith men and without purdah. The ancient finds preserved in Mathura and Lucknow museums depict women without purdah taking part in the Rathayatra processions. The Ajanta frescoes and Mathura sculpture of the Shunga period prove that there was no purdah in those days from the north to the south. We also find that Rajyashri, sister of Harshavardhana, used to participate at the court meetings without any purdah. Lack of purdah is noticed as late as the 12th century AD at the *svayamvara* of Sanyukta, daughter of Jayachanda.

The lack of purdah in those days did not mean that the women enjoyed the same freedom as men. Existence of *antahpuras* (harems) in the palaces is a case in point. Even while accepting women as *bhikshunis*, the Buddha had laid down eight strict rules of conduct for them, one of which was that no *bhikshuni* should herself initiate conversation with a *bhikshu*.[14]

In the Vedic times women used to take part in *sabhas, samitis* and *vidathas*. The Rigveda mentions that the husband desired that the wife should be able to speak at the *vidatha*.[15] Dr. Upadhyaya holds that there used to be a sort of tournament in Vedic times, known as *samana*, consisting of sports, horse and chariot races and shows etc. with equal participation by men and women.[16] Some scholars opine that young men and women used to select their marriage partners at these. It appears that later on, fearing onset of immorality, the leaders of society like, Shvetaketu, framed rigid rules culminating in banning entry of women to the *sabhas*. The *Maitrayani Samhita* (4.7.1) corroborates this by observing that 'for this reason men go to the *vidatha*, and not women'. This, however, did not mean that they were placed in purdah. The examples of Sulabha, Maitreyi, Gargi etc. quoted in an earlier chapter are sufficient to establish this.

However, the *samana* practice could not be completely stopped as we find a variant in the Mauryan period known as '*samaja*' in the famous Buddhist treatise, *Dhammapada*. There used to be a drama festival in the capital, the biggest attraction of which was an artistic dance by a danseuse on a hanging bar. The *Vinayapitaka* mentions a *samaja* in Rajagriha, which became the cause of ruin of a merchant's son, Uggasena. Later on, Ashoka, finding that the practice was degrading the society, put an end to it as evidenced by his Shahbazgarhi rock edict.

Though the royal ladies were confined to the harems in those days, they had full facilities inside for recreation and education etc. Evenso, ordinary women had no purdah. Valmiki describes how hundreds of women saw Rama from their houses when he was entering Ayodhya after vanquishing Ravana. Similarly, according to the *Mahabharata*, many women saw Krishna from their houses as he was entering Hastinapur from Upaplava and hordes of them welcomed him on the road.[17] Mahabharata also mentions that when Arjuna was leaving Hastinapur with the *ashvamedha* horse, a vast concourse of men, women and children surged forward to wish him victory.[18] In the same journey Arjuna, while in Manipur, had found Chitrangada, strolling freely outside. We also hear of rejoicing by the Vrishni and Andhaka men and women on the Raivataka mountain near Dwarka freely.

C.V. Vaidya says that 'in those days widows' could move about freely, but other women had to put on an *uttariya* (a sort of shawl).[19] He further states -"The *Mahabharata* and the *Ramayana* do not mention of Draupadi and Sita being kept in purdah; otherwise Jayadratha and Ravana could not have seen them."[20] The examples are, however, not logical as Ravana had gone before Sita in the garb of a recluse. Even in the recent past of strict purdah women did not avoid appearing before hermits. Similarly, Draupadi could certainly appear before Jayadratha as he was a close relation, being husband of Duryodhana's sister. The position will be clear if we refer to the words uttered by Draupadi before the court to which she had been dragged by Dushshasana—"I have heard that there was an old custom that women were not taken to the *sabhas*. The Kauravas have destroyed that *Sanatana Dharma*."[21] Her words were in keeping with the dictum of the *Maitrayani Samhita* that 'due to that reason only men go to the *sabha*, not women.'

The reason for strict guard over harems was the desire to prevent looseness of character among the inmates. We find that during the period of exile of the Pandavas with Virata, Kichaka had been able to unsuccessfully molest Draupadi (in the guise of Sairandhri) only because being the Queen's brother, he had free access to the *antahpura*. Similarly, *Nalopakhyana* in *Mahabharata* mentions that when Nala had managed to enter the harem and ask Damayanti to marry any of the gods Indra, Varuna etc., the first question raised by Damayanti was -"How were you able to enter? The harem is heavily guarded. And the punishment is very severe."[22] Similarly, there was strict guard over the palace at Nishadha. Nala, the banished King of Nishadha, refers to it in his wanderings thus— "My beloved Queen, whom even wind and sun could not see in the palace, is today sleeping on the floor of an empty public hall like an orphan."[23]

The confinement of women to harems must have been limited to the royal palaces or to the households of the prosperous. But even there the women were frequently allowed to witness ceremonies. The *Mahabharata* says—

"Separate enclosures were erected for women to witness the competition organized by Dronacharya to test the Kauravas and Pandavas."[24] It further describes how women of all *varnas* had gathered in large numbers to witness the show. All this would point to lack of purdah in those days.

References

1. Manusmiti, 3.
2. Manusmiti, 3.53.
3. Mahabharata, Anushasana Parva, 45.20.
4. *Ibid.*, 42.18.19.
5. Baudh. Dh. Shastra,1.2.20.9.
6. Atri Smriti.
7. Padma Purana.
8. Mahabharata, Drona Parva, 73.42.
9. *Ibid.*, Adi Parva, 113.9.10.11.
10. Dr. Altekar: The Position of Women in Hindu Civilization, p. 41.
11. Ghosh:Bharat ka Prachina Itihasa, p. 93.
12. Raghuvansha of Kalidasa, 6.80-81.
13. Ghosh:Bharat ka Prachina, p. 183.
14. Vinaya Pitaka, Chulla Vagga 10.
15. Reg. 10.85.26.
16. V.S.Upadhyaya: Women in Rigveda.
17. Mah, Bh., Udyoga Parva, 84.14.
18. *Ibid.*, Ashvamedha Parva.
19. C.V.Vaidya: Mahabharata Mimamsa, p. 284 (Translation by Madhava Rao Sapre).
20. *Ibid.*
21. Mahabharata, Sabha Parva, 69.9.
22. *Ibid.*, Vana Parva, 55.21.
23. Mahabharata, Vana Parva, 62.21.
24. *Ibid.*, Adi Parva, 134.15-18.

17

The Practical Aspect of Freedom of Women in Society

There is a statement in the *Manusmriti* that "every man should endeavour that the women in the household are kept under control. The father should control the woman before marriage, the husband in youth and the son in her old age, for women do not deserve freedom."[1] This has been a subject of severe criticism of Indian culture. Here we must emphasize at the outset that even though *Manusmriti* had a prime role in guiding Indian society and culture, it was not its sole representative. In the previous chapters we have analysed the role of women on the basis of the testimony in the *Vedas* and other established sources of our culture and had found that they had complete freedom to express themselves in many fields of knowledge and creativity. Therefore, a judicious criticism of the provisions in the *Smritis* is possible only against this background.

On the subject of freedom for women we generally come across two schools of thought. One is the fundamentalists who go by the letter of these provisions. The other comprises those who, without bothering about the inherent spirit, revel in castigating these framers of laws. Both are far from the truth on account of their prejudices. With the stabilization of the Vedic society women are seen to be completely free in all walks of life. This freedom, in due course, gave rise to licentiousness, which forced the social law makers to set limits to this freedom. It was certainly not due to a male bias, but with the good of the society at large. As *Manusmriti* has been at the centre of criticism, we shall try to get at the bottom of thinking in this *Smriti*.

Manusmiti says—"Gods dwell where women are worshipped. All rites are in vain where they are not respected."[2] He further says—"The family in which women grieve gets ruined. Where they are happy, they prosper."[3] He directs that "for the good of the family, men should respect the feelings of their womenfolk and keep them satisfied with proper arrangements for their dress, food and ornaments etc., specially on occasions when lack of these might cause them embarassment before others."[4] His conclusion is that "the family where the husband is satisfied with the wife and vice versa, will definitely prosper."[5] And—"Birth of a progeny, religious rites, care of the family, enjoyment and even heaven for self and ancestors—all are dependent on the wife."[6] Or that- "the lucky women responsible for birth of a progeny are like the *griha dipikas; they are devis*."[7] These quotes and many others given elsewhere throw ample light on the thinking in the Manusmriti.

The denial of freedom has been spelt out explicitly when *Manusmiti* says—"A woman must not perform any important task, even at home, independently, be she an adolescent, young or old. She should remain under the father in childhood, under the husband in youth and under the sons, if she is widowed. She must not yearn to live independently and separately from the father, brother or sons, as the case may be, because this gives a bad name to the families."[8] On the subject it will be interesting to note that the old Roman Law had similar provisions. According to Dr. V.S.Agarwal—"In the ancient Roman Law a woman had no independent existence right from childhood to old age and guardianship of father, husband and son was a must.—"[9] *Mahabharata*, too, has similar statements and Tulasidasa also says—"—just as women get spoilt when they are free. "It is rather enigmatic that the same authors have been showering respect on the women and restricting them as above at the same time. It appears, too, that the statements of *Manusmiti* regarding lack of freedom for women have been interpolated at a later stage when the society might have needed such a restriction. It is certainly incomprehensible that they should not be free to perform even household chores independently. In support of this view our history is full of instances of women who were free thinkers and were well versed not only in household chores, but even in spheres held to be reserved for men. We have already cited examples of Vidula, Sita, Savitri, Gandhari, Kunti and Draupadi and many even in the middle ages. Even Rama has said for Sita that he used to consult her in every matter. Even their religious freedom is established from instances of Queens of Vijayapuri (2nd century B.C.), who were devout Buddhists in spite of the fact that the King followed the Vedic religion.[10]

Further, it can not be denied that women are physically weaker than men, and therefore, needing special protection. Hence the provision of their protection by men can not be treated as a slur on their character. It appears that the main critics, the so called protagonists of women's liberation, are not really concerned about preservation of character. On the other hand, our culture has always been stressing on the purity of the race. Arjuna had feared that the war would lead to killing of myriads of men, that widows would lose their character and that hybrids would be born and so on.[11] Manu was concerned with the character of women of all *varnas* stating that 'women of all *varnas* are to be protected at all cost.'[12] This protection was not merely physical, it was primarily in the context of character. Even *pativratas* for that matter needed protection from evil elements. Thus, Bhishma, while on the bed of arrows had advised that 'women need protection constantly. There are two types of women—saintly and wicked. The saintly ones are *lokamatas* and are responsible for smooth functioning of the world. The wicked ones are sinful and destroyers of family.'[13] That our *shastras* were seriously concerned with preservation of character of women through curbs on licentiousness and not by curbing their day to day freedom will be clear from the statement in *Manusmriti* that 'protection of women is possible by their association in the family earning and expenditure, observance of rules of purity, performance of religious rites and looking after the husband.'[14]

Our seers had realized that an infatuated man could go to any extent and lose all sense of propriety. That is why *Manusmriti* had to say that 'none should sit on the same *asana* (seat) even with his mother, sister or daughter, if alone, because the senses can make even a wise man blind.'[15] Shrimad Bhagavadgita also gives the same warning.[16]

The *Manusmriti* lays special stress on protection of women as an essential adjunct to social progress. It provides for meticulous security in the *harems* of kings. There used to be strict security at the entrance and the sentries as well as servants used to be eunuchs. Barring old teachers, no non-member could secure entry. In spite of this, cases of entry of undesirable elements did take place.

A story in the *Panchatantra* relates how an architect was able to find entry in the ***harem*** and defile the princess. In the story of Nala in the *Mahabharata* Nala had been able to enter the ***harem*** by duping the sentries. *Manusmiti* was aware that mere provision of strict security was no guarantee for preservation of character in the ***harem*** and had to say— 'women can not be protected merely by keeping them inside the *harems* with reliable guards outside. Only those women are safe who know how to defend themselves.'[17]

There are umpteen examples of how even sages could not remain unaffected by the attraction of woman and how demon-like men did not desist from most heinous behaviour. Against this background it should be no wonder that even orphanages and widow-homes are sometimes found to be centres of immorality, not to talk of interstate gangs engaged in trafficking in women. It is another matter that if men could be perfectly disciplined in matters of sex, the need for curbs would not have arisen, as was the case in the kingdom of Ashvapati. Ashvapati was proud that 'there is no thief in my kingdom—, no morally depraved man. And when there is no depraved man, where was the question of a depraved woman?'[18] Valmiki, too, narrates in the *Ramayana* as to how hundreds of Brahmanas insisted on accompanying Rama to the jungle, saying—'our intellect engrossed in the study of the *Vedas* is guiding us to accompany you. We are confident that our women, while left at home, will be able to maintain their character in our absence.'[19]

Confidence of the Brahmanas in their women narrated above is significant. Similar is the view of Mahatma Gandhi that 'women should move about freely, having confidence that Rama will protect them. It should be remembered that menfolk as a whole are not out to grab them; after all , they are born out of women. Ladies should adopt the attitude of mother and not fear any man just as she does not fear her child. In spite of this, if she does encounter a beastly man, she must rest assured that her own armour of purity will protect her.'[20] This summarises the essence of attitude towards character of women in Indian thought.

References

1. Manusmiti., 9.2.3.
2. *Ibid..*, 3.56.
3. *Ibid.*, 3.57.

4. *Ibid.*, 3.59.
5. *Ibid.*, 3,60.
6. *Ibid.*, 9.28
7. *Ibid..*, 9.26.
8. *Ibid.*, 5.147-50.
9. V.S.Agarwal: Paninikalina Bharatavarsha, p. 100.
10. V.S.Agarwal: Indian Art, p. 297.
11. Gita,1.41-42.
12. Manusmiti., 8.359.
13. Mahabharata, Anushasana Parva 43.19.21.
14. Manusmiti., 9.11.
15. Ibid, 2.215.
16. Shrimadbhagavata., 9.19.17.
17. Manusmiti., 9.12.
18. Chhan. Up., 5.11.5.
19. Val. Ram., Ayodhya Kanda, 45.24.25.
20. Mahatma Gandhi: Autobiography.

18

The Women in the Modern Age

The ancient Indian culture had to struggle hard to retain its identity during the Muslim rule and no serious inroads could be made by the alien culture. Rather, when the invaders accepted India as their own country and home, mutual exchange ensued and in spite of many differences, by and large a new spirit of co-ordination and understanding soon developed. As a result, even though no noticeable addition to the store of knowledge accrued due to adverse circumstances, the spirit of our culture remained intact.

The advent of the Britishers in the 18th century and the contact with the Western civilization that ensued, however, resulted in a virtual cultural black-out. Cultural values started waning with the younger generation getting enamoured of the West, coupled with tightening of political shackles. Many Indians with Western education, bedazzled by the foreign culture, started denigrating their ancient tradition and the everlasting values of our culture. The largest contribution towards this decline was that of English medium of education, which unfortunately is retaining its stranglehold on a powerful section of the society even after decades of Independence. The British rulers had succeeded in creating a class of 'Hindustani Babus' by spreading education through the English medium. They tried their best to plant European culture upon the ruins of Indian culture in order to ensure stability of their rule. They were well aware that towards this end political supremacy alone was not adequate and so they tried to win over the heart and soul of the ruled and thrust their culture on them. The well planned 'mission' of making the Indians 'educated' and 'civilized' through the medium of English in place of Sanskrit and indigenous languages was thus started by them with this end in view towards the third decade of the 19th century Their height of ignorance and hatred of Indian culture will be clear from the vain declaration of Lord Macaulay, who was charged with the spread of English education, that just one almirah in a good European library was sufficient to hold the entire literature of India and Arabia.

It was being impressed upon the youth through English education that the British rule was a boon for India, that India was always devoid of nationalism and that such an education would infuse nationalism into them. The hollowness of this claim was soon witnessed in the shape of partition of the country.[1]

The English educated forgot that the idea of nationalism had been ingrained in the Indian psyche right from the Vedic times. We find that the *Rigveda* was the first in the world to address the earth as 'mother' and to exhort people to strive for '*swarajya*' (independence).[2] The *Yajurveda* prays for a prosperous nation [3] and gives vent to love for '*matribhumi*'(motherland), '*matribhasha*' (mother-tounge), and one's own culture.[4] The *rishi* in the Atharva-veda calls the country as his mother and himself her son[5] and vows to sacrifice his all for her.[6] Our literature has been strengthening the feeling of nationalism and patriotism all along as will be seen from the *Puranas*[7] and writings of Kalidasa[8] and others.

The above view does not, however, negate the benefits accrued to the country through English, nor does it deny granting of due place to it in the educational system. It is certainly needed for international contacts. But Sanskrit and our national language must be given the pride of place to preserve our dignity, culture and traditions.

The poison of this cultural onslaught fast became the root cause of cultural oblivion. This was first recognized by Raja Ram Mohan Roy (1772-1832) and then by Swami Dayananda Saraswati, who laboured hard to awaken the soul of India. Then came the first Struggle for Independence in 1857, which was, however, crushed by the British. The next collective effort was the establishment of the Indian National Congress in 1885, which led the country to Independence in 1947.

The history of this renaissance would be incomplete without recounting the contribution of women who proved that they were no less than men in patriotism and sacrifice. We all know how the Rani of Jhansi had excelled in organizing military manoevres and in sacrificing her life for the country in 1857. It is also a matter of record that many women's societies were set up in the wake of the I.N.C. Hemant Kumari Devi, the leader of first such society established on 25th Jan. 1886 at Shillong, within a month of the founding of the I.N.C, published a Hindi paper, named Sugrihini, whose aim was to unite the Bengalis and Assamese politically and culturally.

Swami Dayanand had already started a movement for spread of the Vedic culture amongst women at a time when women's education was nominal. Later, 'Bharat Ratna' Karve contributed immensely to women's education and so did Ramabai. The establishment of Karve Mahila Vishwavidyalaya was a landmark. So was establishment of Mahila Sadan and *ashram* by Ramabai at Pune. The I.N.C. had paid special attention to women's education right from the beginning and a Sarvadeshik Mahila Sammelan was established. It is pioneering efforts like these which have boosted the number of school and college going girls. Today girls are successfully competing with boys in all branches of Arts and Science, even Engineering and Medical.

The contribution of women in the latter day freedom struggle was more widespread and significant. The high degree of patriotism, courage and spirit of sacrifice shown by the women had been a pleasant surprise even for top leaders of the country. Even before Mahatma Gandhi took over the leadership of the I.N.C. women had helped the revolutionaries in many ways. The revolutionaries had started their violent activities with a view to free the country from the foreign rule at about the same time as the great agitation against partition of Bengal. Prominent among those women who helped them were Sarojini, widowed sister of Swami Prajnanand Saraswati, Vinodini Devi, sister of Jatindra Mukerji, Manorama Majumdar, Dukauri Bala Devi., Nati Bala, Sindhu Bala, Kshiroda Sundari etc. It is a matter of regret that their names are not in the limelight.[9] In a similar context the name of Col. Lakshmi is well known, who had organized a women's corps under the famous I.N.A. of Netaji Subhash Chandra Bose.

The woman power had reached its zenith at the time of Non Cooperation Movement of Gandhiji. Thousands of women helped the men, many of them went to jail due to active participation in the movement, bidding farewell to their sons and husbands. Sarojini Naidu was a prominent marcher in Gandhiji's famous Dandi Yatra. She was not to be outdone by anybody in bravely bearing the *lathis* of the Police and the rigours of the jail life.

In this connection the Civil Disobedience Movement of 1930 needs a special mention. Jawahar Lal Nehru writes—"Practically all of us men were in jail in 1930, when a strange thing happened. Our womenfolk came forward like a flood to continue the struggle, which astonished not only the British Govt., but their menfolk as well. These included lakhs of women from the upper and middle classes, who had been traditionally confined to the households; peasant women and women labourers —rich and poor alike—we did not care for the orders of the government and *lathis* of the Police. – When we heard this in Naini jail, where we had been interned, we were overwhelmed with pride. – Later, my father also joined me in the jail. He told us that initially he was not in favour of young and old women gathering in the streets in scorching summer sun and facing the Police. But noticing their abundant enthusiasm, he did not discourage them. Women of our household had also joined."[10] An idea of participation of women in the Independence movement can be had from the fact that in the Salt Satyagraha of 1932 alone more than 17000 women were arrested (compared to 80000 men), out of whom a large number had taken an active part.

Incidentally, this was a decisive blow to the *purdah* system as well. The same sentiment resulted in a very large number of women taking an active part in helping the victims of the worst earthquake ever of 1934 in Bihar. There were many who had come out of ***purdah*** for the first time and collected foodgrains, clothes and donations for the victims. The contribution of women at the time of earthquake in Quetta and heavy floods in the U.P., Assam and Maharashtra was substantial. The name of Kasturba Gandhi stands as a beacon light in this context.

Women at this time were given a lot of encouragement as will be seen from the examples of the prestigious post of the Congress President going to Annie Besant in 1916 and to Sarojini Naidu in 1925. The tradition has continued after Independence with Indira Gandhi becoming the Congress President. This could be contrasted with the position of women in England, the mother of parliamentary system, where they had to struggle hard to secure franchise as against India where they got it without any effort. This right was secured by women in England in 1918, in France in 1920 and in U.S.A. in 1944. In our country Vijayalakshmi Pandit became a minister in the first Congress Government in U.P. even before Independence. In independent India women enjoy the same rights as men in all respects as enjoined by the Constitution. At present there are women members in the Lok Sabha, Rajya Sabha, State Assemblies and Councils. Women are not only Ministers, Sucheta Kripalani is the Chief Minister of U.P.[11] Indira Gandhi has since become the Prime Minister of the country.[12] After 1961 the number of women members in the Parliament is more than in any Parliament in the world. Our Constitution confers the right to women to become even the President. Sarojini Naidu was the Governor of U.P. and her daughter, Padmaja Naidu, is the present Governor of U.P.[13] Vijaya Lakshmi Pandit has been Ambassador of India in most important countries like, U.S.A. and Russia. It is also a matter of pride for the country that she was the first woman to become President of the U.N. General Assembly.

Women are doing very well as teachers and Principals in colleges and universities and as advocates and judges in courts. Their contribution in the literary field is also substantial. The poetry of Sarojini and Toru Dutt in English has won international acclaim. Toru Dutt has a unique distinction of earning acclaim as a great poetess in a short life span of 21 years. Women have earned fame as writers in the national language Hindi as well as in regional languages. Subhadra Kumari Chauhan and Mahadevi Varma are shining examples. They are also coming up fast in spheres of trade, industry and banking. Recently (1959) when Sumati Morarji was visiting England, a crowd of Britishers had gathered in the Hyde Park of London to see her when they learnt that she was a top name in Industry, being a Director of Scindhia Steam Navigation Co. of India as well as the chairperson of the Indian National Steamship Owners Association.[14]

Indian women rose to the occasion at the time of Chinese aggression in 1962 and Pakistan War in 1965. They even came forward to acquire military training.

To touch upon another important aspect, the tendency amongst some modern women to discard the national dress and to adopt the western attire is not in the national interest. In this connection the warning of Pliny is quite relevant when he told the Romans in the 1st century A.D. that 'every year fifty lakh...[15] were going to India for import of tradeable items, specially cosmetics and dresses etc. He castigated the fashionable women of Rome for constantly looking to India for items of pleasure that were meant to enhance their nude beauty.[16] Similarly, the race amongst the women for taking up jobs is not understood. While it may be necessary for improving family earnings, the tendency to be independent might not be wholesome. This, however, does not apply to women who take up the medical profession due to an urge to serve the society or who run *ashramas* for widows or who take up other real social work suited to their genius. It must not be forgotten that fighting for women's supremacy might be relevant to western social ethos and economy, but it has no place in our tradition and values.

On the subject of women's rights, we have seen that there have been progressive changes in the laws of succession and property rights for women in the past, but the laws which came up after Independence have been far more liberal. In the first category mention could be made of Prevention of *Sati* Act, 1829 and Hindu Widow Remarriage Rule 20 of 1856, referred to elsewhere. Similarly, the Sharda Act (Prevention of Child Marriage Act, 1928) was a notable enactment. Revolutionary changes, however, took place only after Independence. The Hindu Marriage Act 25 of 1955 put an end to many provisions and gave a more comprehensive meaning to the term 'Hindu'. According to this, it covers all those who believe in any form or sect of Hinduism and includes not only Vira Shaivas, Ligayatas, Brahmasamajis, Prarthanasamajis and Aryasamajis, but also Buddhists, Jains and Sikhs. To remove ambiguity it declares that it includes every Indian who is not Christian, Muslim, Parsee, or Jew. This put an end to polygamy by laying down that the marriage would be valid only if the bride or the bridegroom did not have a living spouse already. It also removed all restrictions of caste, *varna, gotra* etc. in regard to legality of marriage. It laid down conditions for a marriage to be illegal. It also provided for divorce, which was a revolutionary step and against the ideals of marriage. Legalisation of *sagotra* and *samapravara* marriages is, however, against the age -old social and religious beliefs.

Divorce has reached disasterous proportions in the West. It is said that in some cities in U.S.A. there are as many divorces as marriages. In Germany divorce cases in courts have risen to forty thousand and amendment in the current laws is being seriously considered. (As in 1961). The main reason for the high incidence is that divorce is being granted on flimsy grounds. Alarmed at this state of affairs, Pope, the religious head of the Catholics, too, has called for a change in the existing laws. Viewed against this background, our fears regarding decline in moral values as a result of a liberal application of the divorce rules can not be called ill-founded.

The other significant Act is the Hindu Succession Act 30 of 1956. In the chapter on *Stree Dhana* and Succession we have seen that there has been progressive enhancement of rights of women, but in this age of equal rights for men and women these were not found adequate. Therefore, through 'The Rights of Women in the Property Act, 1937' a change was brought about that as against the existing right of maintenance only in the undivided Hindu family property, now she could inherit the entire share of the husband on his death; only she could not transfer the same. The widow is also to get equal share in the property of a Hindu dying without writing a will as the sons, daughters, etc. Just as in the case of divorce, here too, the sections of the Act that provide for share to the women in the property on the mother's side as well (under certain conditions) could lead to bickerings and discord and dismantling of the joint family.

In the end it will be justified to say that women have been contributing substantially to the attainment of the four *purusharthas* enshrined in Indian culture and that they have been forging ahead in different directions. No doubt, in the process, certain undesirable trends have been coming up, yet this is a usual feature of transition, which could soon disappear in the light of genuine culture. There is a great future for our women!

References

1. Rigveda 10.18.10.
2. *Ibid.*, 5. 66.6.
3. Yoju, 20.43.
4. *Ibid.*, 20.43.
5. Athar., 12.
6. *Ibid.*, 12.1.54.
7. Vishnu Purana 2.3.24.
8. Kumara Sambhava, 71.1.
9. Dainik Az, 'Swadinata Visheshanka'. p. 21, dt. 15.8.61.
10. Jawahar Lal Nehru: *Discovery of India*, p. 32 (In Author's words).
11. This refers to near about 1961 when the book (in Hindi) was first published.
12. Refers to 1981 when the second edition came out (in Hindi).
13. This refers to near about 1961 when the book (in Hindi) was first published.
14. *Northern India Patrika*, 29th June 1959, p. 4.
15. Coin of Roman Empire, valued at about 1.5 rupees.
16. Pliny the Elder (C. 23-79 AD): Historica Naturalist (Natural History in 37 Books III-VI, Geography and Ethnology). See Warmington, The Commerce of Ancient Rome with India.

19

Comparative Position of Women in World Civilizations

A comparative study of position of women in ancient civilizations, in tribes as well as in world religions is both interesting and revealing. We give here a brief outline of the same.

Other Ancient Civilizations: Greece, Egypt, Rome, Semitics, Primitive Semitics, Babylon, Assyria and Sumer, Abyssinia, Persia, China, Japan, Korea.

World religions: Christianity, Islam, Judaism

Ancient Tribes and Races: Celtic Tribes, Slavic Tribes, Teutonic Races.

India Most of the details in regard to civilizations, other than Indian, given hereunder have been collected from the Encyclopedia of Religion and Ethics, Edinburgh 1908 (edited by James Hastings.)

Other Ancient Civilizations

Greece

In ancient Greek civilization marriage was entered into with a religious perspective for the purpose of continuing lineage as well as from a utilitarian angle of maintaining a household. The laws of Athens do not shed light on the extent of respect given to women. Monogamy was the general rule, though polygamy was also in vogue. The citizens of Athens were prohibited from marrying foreigners, but they could purchase a foreign husband or wife as a slave. Mistresses were common.

There were very few restrictions regarding marriage and the laws of succession to property etc., were such as to encourage incestual marriage. Only marriage between siblings was taboo. According to Aristotle, in the beginning men used to purchase wives and the Epic is full of descriptions of the sale of brides. The system of dowry was started in Athens in the historical period, and it became a symbol of status.

Men were free to divorce their wives, causing immense hardship to them. There was no joint property between husband and wife. Many women remained unmarried all their life. No legal action was needed for divorce. The husband could simply send his wife back to her parents along with the dowry brought by her. The wife had, however, recourse to Archons (courts) for this purpose. Divorce was possible first by mutual consent.

If the wife had no issue of her own or an adopted one, she could remarry after divorce. There was a time in Athens when it was a criminal offense for a married woman to have sex with a man other than her husband. The same went for married men, but only in respect to married women. Later on, unmarried women and widows were also included in this. If the husband of the lax woman was able to catch his wife's lover red-handed, he could kill him on the spot or could impose a minor punishment or fine on him. If, however, the lover could not be caught or would not admit the offense, it was incumbent on him to institute a case of Thesmothetae (obstruction) in the court against the husband. If he failed to prove his case, he was handed over to the husband of his lover who then had the right to punish him. If the fault of the woman was proved, the husband was forced to sever his relations with her and she was barred entry to temples. There was no provision for inflicting bodily or capital punishment on such women.

Though not much is known about the thinking of Greeks (other than Athenians), it is certain that infidelity was considered a crime everywhere, as proved from the statement of Xen Hiero that in many cities such a man was killed by the citizens with impunity. Similarly the lawmaker of Lokia, Zaleucus, had ruled that the man accused should be bled to death. In Cyme and Picidia the woman was taken and seated on an ass. In other cities like Leprione, Gortin, and Tinirose, etc. such criminals were either fined, divested of their franchise, or stoned.

Education of women was rare. However, we do find cases of cultured women. The fidelity of Semo and Penelope and Antiocle's love for the sister has become legendary. According to Ecleciasueus of Aristophanes, women had a big say in administration. The great thinker, Plato, in his famour book 'Republic' considers women inferior to men due to physical weakness for purpose of state administration, but he generally advocateds equality.

Egypt

The avilable records regarding marriage matters are so scant that it is difficult to establish the extent to which blood relationship was followed. Later on, the Pharoahs married their own sister or god-sisters. In the Egypt of Roman times such marriages were common in society. Child marriage was also common. Adultery by a married women was considered a sin.

Respect for parents was stressed in those times. It was the custom to pour water for the dead parents, who were believed to be resting in the Vally of Death. The mother enjoyed greater respect than the father. In royalty succession went to the mother's side. Bringing forth a son was considered a very important duty. It was also incumbent upon men to love their wives and look after them well. Polygamy, though not prohibited, was rare. Divorce depended on the will of the husband, but he had to pay compensation, if it was on inadequate grounds. Promiscuity in society was rampant. It is clear from the warning of Morlitz—'to beware of unknown women. A woman, staying separately from her husband, is like a bottomless ocean.'

The wife was free to manage her property and will the same. There are cases of several queens who had ruled the kingdom as per a will successfully.

Rome

In the prehistoric age marriage by force was the vogue in Italian tribles. Later on, marriage by purchase of the bride became common. In those days marriage had two purposes- security of the household and birth of progeny. The children born from mistresses did not enjoy citizenship.

In the historic age, marriage among the colaterals up to seventh generation was banned. The consent of parents was essential for marriage. The marriageable age was generally twelve years for girls and fourteen years for boys. It is noteworthy that the daughter of the famous Cicero was married at the age of ten. The bride brought a dowry and controlled the slaves of the household. In religious and domestic affairs her husband consulted her, though not in intellectual and political matters. Generally she was not permitted to leave the house without the permission of her husband or without a guard.

Towards the last days of the Republic, the conduct of women became very lax. The divorce system began and it was very easy to obtain the same, which resulted in the onset of polygamy. Of course, this did not necessarily mean that immorality was invariably there. Records show that Pompeii married five times, Caesar four times, Cicero three times and Pliny II also three times, though all of them were known to be of good character.

However, the ideals of sexual relationships in that age were not high. Intercourse by a woman with another man was considered immoral, but the same thing done by a man was treated only as a misdemeanor. Intercourse with an unmarried woman was a common occurrence. Later, in the days of the Roman Empire immorality was at its peak and Augustus Caesar had to declare adultery by the wife or the mistress a cognizable offense.

Thinkers like Cicero were dissatisfied with the lax moral standards; because materialism and promiscuity had crossed all limits. But towards the end of Roman empire, in the time of Constantine, a major change took place in moral standards based on personal conduct as a result of contact with principles of Greek philosophy and Eastern thought. According to the Constitution of 'Twelve Tables,' the husband had complete authority over the wife, just as over the daughter. Later on, women attained a bit higher status. Earlier, women did not enjoy succession rights, but under the new dispensation this gradually came up.

Semitics

According to most sociologists the early Semitics considered marriage a temporary union of a man and a woman and sexual lapses existed as in most primitive societies. There were interesting changes in this situation off and on.

(i) Primitive Semitics

Their original home was Arabia. Marriage was temporary. Divorce was very common in all Semitic countries, especially Arabia and Abyssinia. There were marriages, which could be called a mixture of polyandry and polygamy. In due course, a custom of "Mutta" sprang up in which marriage was limited only to three nights, and this continued until the advent of the Prophet Muhammad. According to Stralio, the wife used to be a common property of the family; she belonged to all men in the family and the eldest among the men used to be the master. A person belonging to another family, if accused of adultery involving such a family, was killed.

(ii) Babylon, Assyria and Sumer

Prior to Hammurabi's Constitution and before the first Babylonian dynasty (2128 - 1924 B.C.) marriage was performed without rituals. According to the prevalent custom marriage of one man with one woman was considered proper, but at the same time the man could keep mistresses and produce children through them. The husband could divorce the wife after providing for her maintenance. The wife also had a right to divorce. Dowry and sale of bride were both legal. The son also inherited the father's mistresses.

The Sumerian texts written prior to Hammurabi containing rules for the family continued to be followed. According to one of these, if a mother told her son that he was not actually her son, he would renounce the house and all his belongings. If a married woman disowned her husband, she would be thrown into the river. But if a married man did the same, he had only to give half a 'maina'silver to the woman. There were, however, rules for protection of married women against excesses by the husband as well as for the widows and orphaned children. Drinking and promiscuity reached such extremes that intercourse on public roads had become common. In a nutshell, the moral standards of the Babylonians, like their religious beliefs, were entirely materialistic and based on gratification of senses.

In the early stages of Semitic civilization the woman had the right to select her man. She could call such a man to her father's house and live with him as long as she liked.

However, children born out of such union were not considered legal.[1]

In the present custom in vogue in Semitic societies the bride goes to the groom's house, for which the groom's father pays "Mehr" as bride price. Women so purchased through Mehr could be temporarily exchanged as well. Their definition of adultery is peculiar. It is valid if committed in the knowledge of the husband.

The Code of-Hammurabi brought about some improvement in the status of women that existed prior to 2250 B.C. According to this, marriage was confirmed through a contract. If a person committed adultery with a woman living in parent's house after engagement, he was sentenced to death, but the woman went scot free. If the engagement was with a stepson of her father and marriage had not been consummated, the adulterer was simply punished with a fine of half-a 'maina'silver. The woman, in such a case, was divested of her property and made free to marry elsewhere. Marriage was settled by the parents. On the death of the husband, the widow would marry her husband's younger brother and the first-born child was treated as that of the deceased. Divorce was very easy for the husband. In a nutshell, the punishment for adultery was severe for women, but not for men.

(iii) Abyssinia

Like the Hebrews, Abyssinia upheld the custom of the widow marrying her husband's younger brother. Mistresses were common and approved of in Christianity as well and many of the ancient Semitic customs are now in vogue.

Persia

The ancient Zoroastrian religion of Iran lay great sanctity on family ties, which is gleaned from the declaration in Vendidada that 'the second happiest place in the world is that where a noble soul establishes his family.[4] This resembles the saying in the *Manusmriti* that 'all *ashramas* are dependent on *grihasthashrama*!' The Gathas of this religion preach leading of a holy life by the husband and wife and helping each other in performance of good deeds. Marriage has been held to be a religious duty and helping in the marriage of a poor girl, a meritorious act. The Avesta lays down the age of marriage as fifteen years.

The consent of the bride before the priest is a must. Due to no ban on *sapinda* marriages the same between paternal cousins is permissible.

Adultery was considered a dreadful sin in ancient Persia. The *Gatha Ushtaveti* warns against adultery. *Yojota Ashinama* declares that 'it is the worst of sins for men to seduce virgins for adultery. Both such men and women are enemies of the good Earth and are like beasts' They called unmarried women of character Iridata Fidri and treated them as icons of good morals. They worshipped the presiding deity for protection against Jahi, the symbol of adultery. Faithfulness to the husband is the prime duty of a woman. She should worship her husband and obtain orders from him every morning regarding what she should do that day. In the later-Gatha period the women attained equality with men and also secured the right to worship Ahura Mazda (Almighty God).

China

The basis of moral behavior was mostly the teachings of Confucius (6th Century B.C.). These ordained service of parents by the children and burying them after death with honours. Obedience to mother was stressed.

The wife was kept under the husband all the time. "She was always dependent before marriage, on father or elder brother; after marriage, on husband and if widowed; on her son." Her field of activity was limited to the household. Respecting her father-in-law, service of husband and rearing children were her religious duty. Marriage was considered a primary duty in life. The women were held very high in the domain of love. Divorce was easy for the husband. But if her parents were not alive or she was from a low class or poor, she could not be divorced. The protection of widows was an essential duty.

Japan

There are three stages of the custom of marriage in the not so ancient Japan—(1) Tai Horyo age (701-1192 A.D.) in which the influence of the Chinese constitution and code of conduct is clearly visible, (2) the age of nobles (from the end of the 12th century A.D. until Migi age, and (3) the present age, influenced by Christianity. Here marriage is a contract, requiring agreement of both families. Until Migi age the parents used to enter into this contract and consent of the groom and the bride was not necessary. Even though there is no caste system, there is a clan of people who continued to be considered lowly and marriage with them was not possible.

In the Tai Horyo age, the age of marriage was fifteen and thirteen years for the groom and bride respectively. According to ancient Japanese law polygamy was prohibited, but there was no limit for mistresses. Divorce was legal and widows could remarry upon the death of the husband and vice versa. Faithfulness of the wife was commendable as will be gleaned from the saying 'that a faithful wife does not look to more than one husband.' There was no dearth of women who upon receiving the news of their husband's death in the field of battle would get their head shaved, or who would become a priest or even become a *sati* by committing suicide. In due course there was a decline in this type of devotion towards the husband. The men or women had no right to marry again in the case of divorce or punishment for adultery. Marriage between paternal relatives was permissible.

In ancient Japan the husband had unlimited rights over the wife, '*streedhana*'(personal property of the wife) was nominal and women owning any property or moneys, barring their children and ornaments, were rare. The passing of Civil Code (1896-98) enhanced the rights of women.

The oldest religion of Japan is Shinlo or Chintaism (a Chinese word meaning Way of Gods.) Its major characteristic is obedience to parents and elders. Confucianism and Buddhism arrived in Japan in 284 A.D. and 552 A.D. respectively and cast a great influence on the Japanese way of life. Under the influence of Mahayana Buddhism adultery was prohibited completely.

Korea

The boy and the girl had no say in their marriage, which was settled by the father, grandfather, or elder brother. Child marriage was in vogue in spite of law to the contrary. The age of the bride and the groom at the time of marriage was generally twelve to thirteen years respectively. Though marrying for a second time was not prohibited, it was considered derogatory. The husband had the right to divorce, which could not be refused by the wife.

World Religions

Christianity

The New Testament ordained that the wife must obey the husband and the two should love and care for each other. It accepts authority of the husband over the wife. In the Old Testament polyandry was not prohibited and it was common in old Israel. But in the post-exile period the Jewish preachers laid down that monogamy was ideal. According to the New Testament, a man must marry only one woman and vice-versa and produce children for the continuance of the race.

The Jews, Romans and to some extent the Greeks, where the relationship between the wife and husband was more or less like the master and the slave, believed in little contact with their wife other than sexual. This led to illicit love affairs and the married woman's status deteriorated. The Romans and Greeks generally behaved alike in this regard. In spite of the Jewish Constitution being different, Jews were influenced by the Gentiles' principlelessness and moral behavior declined. The New Testament clearly condemned such relationships and the Gospels declared divorce to be sinful. In ancient Rome divorce was considered derogatory and-inauspicios and they prided themselves for 520 years that they had no custom of divorce. But Jewish law legalized divorce.

Though Christianity considers marriage to be a holy rite, in the eyes of law it is a contract, due to which divorce ends the marriage completely and the husband and wife are left free to remarry elsewhere. But the Christian fathers consider divorce to be just a separation, because according to them, marriage is unbreakable. That is why even after divorce, they do not permit remarriage. But the reformists favoured unfettered divorce. Even so, there are many Roman Catholic countries where divorce is prohibited by law. According to them, it is a must to consider blood relationship, marriage relationship and spiritual affinity. Therefore, no marriage is possible between foster child and foster father or between any two persons who may be a foster parent and a foster child.

In the Seventh Commandment in the Sermon on the Mount, Christ preaches: "Thou shall not covet the neighbour's wife. Thou shall not commit adultery." This teaching was meticulously followed in Africa and Italy in the 2nd Century AD But with the waning of the initial enthusiasm in the spread of the new religion, discipline had to be slackened. In the early days of Christianity there was stress on the equality of husband and wife. Aquinas highlighted this aspect of equality and laid down that the woman had full right to marry or not, regardless of the wishes of her parents. Reformation, however, considered that marriage made life meaningful and that its consistency was service of God Himself. Adultery was laid down as sufficient ground for divorce and the innocent party was given the right to remarriage.

The writings of Shiler, J.M. Fichte, Schleismachi, and Evethe went a long way in securing proper place to the woman in the household and the society. But, on the other hand, the philosopher Schopenhaur gave his view that women were created for obeying orders and that they must be kept under control, as they, by nature, needed a guardian at all times.

Islam

In the Semitic Arabia, prior to the Prophet Mohammed a man could keep any number of free mistresses. The Prophet limited this number to four. But even he did not limit the number of slave mistresses. The changes he made included prohibition of marriage with one's mother, daughter, biological sister, aunt, or niece, maternal grandmother, mother-in-law, step-sister and daughter-in-law. Adultery by women was considered a crime, but not clearly so for the men. The Muslims were also free to divorce the wife like the Hebrews.

In Islam adultery is viewed very adversely. The Koran (Sura 24-1.5) orders, "both the man and woman committing adultery should be caned a hundred times and no mercy should be shown as per 'this religion of Allah.' If a person accused a virtuous woman of adultery and was unable to produce four witnesses, he was to be caned a hundred times. (There is however, some dispute regarding whether persons committing adultery were to be stoned to death or merely caned as above.) But the second Caliph ruled that in Islam punishment for adultery was death by stoning. The Islamic law provides for stoning and caning in such cases. At the same time the compulsory provision of the requirement of four men witnesses in cases of adultery made it nearly impossible to be proved in actual practice. It also holds that the husband has the right to kill both the wife and her lover, if caught red-handed. Further, if the husband suspects his wife of infidelity, he is not bound to produce witnesses. He has merely to declare her infidelity on oath. Then if the wife just takes an oath of fidelity, she is not punished, the marriage is annulled.

In Islam women are kept in harems and they have no freedom at all. The Prophet Mohammed raised the status of women beyond what it was in ancient Arabia. She was given right of succession to property and was no longer treated as property to be passed on in succession. Further, free women could not be forced into marriage. If a woman remarried after Talaq (divorce) the ex-husband was not entitled to get back from the ex-wife whatever she had received from him. Women of higher class could study poetry and arts etc., and even teach. But in general, mutual contact and education was not for the ordinary class. Purdah was the rule of the day.

Judaism

The Jews believe that every person must marry and that those who do not do so harm the handiwork of God and drive away divinity from the land of Israel due to their misdeeds. They consider a happy household as the outcome of marriage and the sign of a good family man. They do not consider parents' permission essential for the marriage of grown-up children. For a long time the Jews felt that marriage at an early age helped in preserving morality. They considered the marriageable age as thirteen and eighteen for the bride and groom respectively.

Polygamy is not prohibited for the Jews, but monogamy is the usual practice. Marriage between paternal cousins is permitted. Though upholding the right of the husband over the wife, the Jew nevertheless exhibits respect for her and, as proof, narrates the stories of virtuous women every Friday evening religiously. This is similar to the narrative amongst the Hindus at the time of marriage.

Sex between a married woman and a man other than her husband and vice versa is considered a crime, but not so for a man with an unmarried woman. The prevailing penal code in this regard was amended to provide for divorce of the adulteress and ceasing of rights accrued to her on marriage. The man was to be flogged. The rules provided for forcing the husband to divorce the fallen wife and prevent her from marrying her love. Similarly on the petition of the wife against the husband for adultery, provision was made for forcing the husband to grant divorce. In times to come adultery and incest were ranked among major crimes.

Ancient Tribes and Races

Celtic Tribes

In Celtic tribes marriage was based on political considerations. The custom of bride price existed. In ancient Ireland the father of the bride used to take the entire Coibche (bride price) in one instalment. Later on, whenever the woman got married, half of the Coibche went to the father and the other half to her. In Scotland the father of the bride used to take her to the king for the first night before the marriage. Adultery was widespread and divorce was possible on flimsy grounds. The husband could keep any number of mistresses. The wife, though much higher in status than the mistresses, was not equal to the husband. In ancient Britain and Ireland polyandry was quite common and one woman could be wife to as many as ten or twelve husbands, generally all brothers. The children thus born were considered to be those of the first husband. In Ireland things were so slack that adultery with others' mothers, wives, and sisters was not considered improper. Women were considered to be the property of men in Caledonia as well. Before the spread of Christianity polygamy was also common. There was no restriction of sapinda (same lineage) or sub-caste etc. Marriage within the family was fully prevalent in Ireland. Princess Clauderin, who had been wife to three of her brothers, later on married her own son Luged, the King.[3] In mediaeval times polygamy was banned in Wales and Britanny. The position of women amongst the Gauls was horrible. Men were fond of wars and their women used to look after agriculture and, after marriage, were forced to lead an amorous life.

The custom of marriage within the family was prevalent in Wales as well. The husband was the sole owner of the household, including the wife. If she ever spoke harshly to her husband, she had to pay a fine. If the husband so chose, he could cane her thrice in place of the fine. The husband had the right to take the lives of his children until they were the age of thirteen. In the early stages there was no system of marriage in Scotland. In the tribes of northern Scotland women jointly belonged to men who generally were brothers, or father and sons.[4]

Slavic Tribes

There were two types of marriages prevalent amongst the ancient Slavs - by forcibly bringing a girl from another clan and by purchase. The custom of marrying a girl by force is prevalent even now amongst the southern Slavs (Yugoslavia.)

Teutonic Races

The Germans and Anglo-Saxons comprise of the Teutonic races. The Germans have been considered ideal in regard to moral standards of husband and wife right from the time of Tacitus. Polygamy was rare and limited to cases of desire to establish relations with the high-ups. Examples like that of King Harold Fairhair who had several queens were rare. The anecdotes of Iceland tell us that divorce on flimsy grounds was, however, common over there. Tacitus also mentions of some women who had been punished for adultery. But later authors, mostly of Iceland and Norway, do not mention any such punishment for women while they talk of heavy fines on the lovers. According to the old laws of Norway the punishment for adultery was the same for both.

According to Tacitus, 'the wife does not keep herself aloof from the desire for good deeds as well as from the dangers of war.'[5] We hear of women who successfully helped the soldiers in the battlefield. The women in those days did not drink, though men did so.

India

The comparison with women around the world fully determines the position of women in India. Nevertheless, before closing we shall analyze the salient features. The preceding chapters highlight the fact that right from the Rigvedic age the Indian society had been evolving along a pattern in which both men and women have been exhorted to achieve the highest goal. In the well known set up of four *ashramas* the highest achievement for an individual was this realization. The Indian society has not slipped from this goal in its life of thousands of years, marked by changes and vicissitudes. We do not find this characteristic anywhere else.

In the scheme of *grihasthashrama* we notice several factors where the Indian culture excels other cultures. We find evidence of thousands of Indians, including women, who have led a life of celibacy and morality unlike in other cultures. Even so, the established social system is rooted in *grihasthashrama* based on marriage.

No other society has as lofty and pure ideals for marriage as in India. Here the goal of marriage has been to fulfil God's desire and pursue *dharma* through bringing forth of progeny. That is why marriage has not been considered a contract, but a religious rite, which is believed to maintain the tie even after death. It is because of religiosity that the idea of *kanyadana* was developed in which the girl is required to remain a virgin before marriage. No other culture has got this concept.

Some religions, other than Hinduism, have also developed high ideals of marriage. For example, ideals of marriage among the Zoroastrians of ancient Persia are seen to be establishment of a pure family life as a religious duty. The Jews find fulfilment of God's desire in contracting marriage for a happy family life. Christianity considers marriage to be a religious rite and unbreakable, but in the eyes of their law it is only a contract. In ancient Rome in the beginning marriage was for defence of the nation through progeny and for running the household. But subsequently it was held to be a life long companionship of the man and the wife and a fusion of heavenly and earthly duties. In China marriage was ordained to be a primary duty of man, but it is not clear as to what its aim was. Similarly in ancient Greece though marriage was considered a religious duty, its aim was only running the household and bringing forth children.

Elsewhere, we find no high ideals of marriage, but only satisfaction of sexual impulses, and at the most, regulation of the same. For example, before the advent of Islam, marriage had no other purpose amongst the Semitics than satisfaction of sexual impulses, and they considered it to be a temporary union with full scope for license. The Semitic tribes of Babylon and Assyria before Hammurabi had no practice of religious rites of marriage and due to the lack of any ideals the wife could be transferred to others by the husband.

The rules regarding prohibited marriages have also been different in other cultures. Practically everywhere marriage within the same family line was permitted in contrast to Indian society. In ancient Greece some marriages were, no doubt, prohibited but their number was negligible. In Egypt marriage; even between brother and sister or uncle and niece' was not prohibited. In Rome, in the early days there was a restriction in marriage up to seven generations in the family line. But later, this restriction was removed. Marriage within the family line was not prohibited amongst the Jews and it was permitted between paternal cousins, but the later reforms stopped such marriages. In ancient Iran, where there was no restriction on *sapinda* marriages, even real paternal cousins could intermarry. Similarly, before the advent of Christianity there was no prohibition os *sapinda* marriages amongst Celtic tribes. In Japan only children of the same parents could not intermarry; there was no such restriction for other close relations. The number of prohibited marriages in Islam is fairly large, but even there marriage within the family line is permitted in several cases. Amongst the Roman Catholics the restrictions are based on blood relationships, certain marriage relationships and on spiritual considerations. Accordingly, marriage between 'god father' and 'god daughter' or between any two persons who have the same 'god father' or 'god mother' was considered invalid.

But in Indian culture due to restrictions on widow marriage and divorce the question of marriage with a woman who had been married earlier did not arise. Further; not only marriage in the same family line is prohibited, it is also not permitted within the same '*gotra*' and '*pravara*'. Also, marriage between two persons who are related on the paternal side within seven generations and on the maternal side, within five generations is not permitted. In addition, even though *anuloma* and *pratiloma* marriages were not prohibited amongst Brahmanas and Kshatriyas in Vedic times, all *asavarna* (not belonging to same *varna*) marriages were totally banned subsequently. We do not find such efforts to avoid hybrid progeny in any other culture.

Another point for comparison is the relationship between the man and the wife. In Egypt there was a direction for loving the wife and her maintenance. In Islam there is a direction of mutual fidelity. In the New Testament of Christians the husband and the wife are considered complementary to each other. There is a direction for mutual love and for obedience on the part of the wife to the husband. The Jews also accept the husband's authority over the wife. The wife is directed to serve the husband, rear the children and run the household. The husband is directed to love the wife. The Zoroastrianism of ancient Iran directs that husband and wife lead a holy life and help each other in the performance of noble deeds and that the wife must worship the husband and remain true to him. In Greece, where women as a class were considered inferior to men, there is no evidence that the wife enjoyed the love and respect of the husband. In ancient Wales the husbands tortured the wives and were even entitled to kill their children younger than fourteen years of age.

The evolution of ideals of relationships between husband and wife has, however, been unique in Indian society. In laying down requirement of fidelity, it has prescribed devotion of the wife towards the husband and monogamy for the husband. Further, though acknowledging the dependence of the wife on the husband, the couple is considered to be complementary to each other. The wife is considered to be *ardhangini* (one half of the husband's body) and no religious rite is complete without her. The husband is responsible for the maintenance and protection of her body and character. Neither the husband nor the wife can leave each other under any circumstances. Both are required to be patient and considerate to each other. Along with the direction for the wife to serve the husband, there is unmistaken requirement for the husband to respect the wife and treat her like a friend and to make her a party in consultations.

However, due to there being no prohibition on polygamy in India, the social structure has been male based, in spite of the ideal of monogamy and the practice of plural marriages for the husband has been in vogue right from the ancient days. According to the Old Testament, polygamy was not prohibited, but the New Testament had laid a complete ban on this. Polygamy was not prohibited in Egypt and it grew in the Republican Rome. It was prevalent among the Celtic tribes before the spread of Christianity. In the Semitic countries – Arabia and Assyria – the man could take any number of wives. Prophet Mohammad, however, limited this number to four, which continues. In Korea and Japn even though it is prohibited, there is not restriction on mistresses. In Burma, though not prohibited, it is considered derogatory in higher society.

In Indian society the mroal standards in regards to adultery are very lofty and unique. Here it is enforced upon a man to treat a women, other than his wife, as mother and adultery is considered a sin as well as a cognizable offense under all circumstances.

As against this, earlier in ancient Athens it was a cognizable offence for a married woman to have sex with another man and a married man to do so with the wife, sister or mother of an Athenian citizen or with a citizen's mistress, if she was a born of citizen of Anthens. Beyond this sex was not illegal. Later on, sex with an unmarried woman or a widow also became an offence. In ancient Eqypt there was hardly any restriction on premartial sex. Sex with a married woman was considered a crime; but there was no mention as to whether it was so in other cases. Sexual morality was very lax in Roman Republic. Adultery was a crime for the woman, but not so for the man. Sex with unmarried women was very common. For the Jews fidelity is a must, but sex with an unmarried woman was not unusual. There is lot of similarity between Zorostrianism of ancient Iran and Indian society in this respect. There, too, extramarital sex is considered sinful and a cognizable offence for both men and women. They too, place a chaste unmarried woman and a faithful wife on a high pedestal. Islam condemns adultery and provides for severe punishment for the same without showing any mrecy. In it the husband has been given the right to kill both the wife and the lover, if caught red-handed. However, sex with the maid is not considered adultery.

Adultery among the Celts, where there was a custom for the bride to spend her first night with the King; was rampant. In Japan adultery became sinful after the advent of Mahayana Buddhism (552 A.D.). Amongst the Hebrews, there is insistence on faithfulness for the wife, but not so for the husband; and there is no moral binding for unmarried women. In ancient Semites the concept of sex was animal-like; the woman was free to have sex with anybody merely after informing the husband.

Divorce had no place in the ideals of marriage in Indian society. All other societies provide for this, though with varying rights for men and women. In Greece the husband could divorce the wife without taking recourse to law, but the wife could not do so. In Egypt the husband could freely divorce his wife; he had only to pay compensation if there were no plausible grounds. In Rome divorce was considered derogatory in the beginning, but it became quite rampant in the Republican period. In Babylon and Assyria the couple were free to divorce at will. Amongst the Hebrews, with the promulgation of Hammurabi's laws whereas the husband could freely divorce the wife, the latter had to face several hurdles. Among the Celts the couple could freely divorce each other. In China the husband could divorce the wife, but there is no evidence that the wife could do so. In Japan divorce is permitted, but neither the husband nor the wife could marry again. In Korea the husband could divorce the wife freely and the wife could not refuse. In Islam merely pronouncing Talaq three times by the husband is adequate for divorce. But for the same purpose the wife has to go to the court. She is permitted to marry again after a certain period. The Roman Catholics have no provision for divorce. It is, however, permitted for other Christians. The Jewish law also treats divorce valid

In contrast, as mentioned earlier, woman was held in high esteem in India due to the dictum that she was never to be slain and that she was to be treated in the household like a deity or a queen. Their inherent ability to delve deep into knowledge and creativity were fully recognized. *pativratya* (devotion to the husband) has been a unique feature of Indian women, which has led them to be treated as an embodiment of the Adi Shakti (Primordial Power).

References

1. Robertson Smith: History of Ethics and Morality, pp. 78-79.
2. Vendidada, 3.2.
3. Book of Linster 23, Col. 2.
4. Keen, p. 3.138.
5. Gorin, 28.

1. Dancing Girl, Bronze, Mohen-jo-daro, Pakistan.

2. Chauri-bearer (Yakshi), Limestone, Didarganj, Bihar.

3. Stone Railing, Bharhut, Madhya Pradesh.

4. Sanchi Stupa No. 1, Yakshi, Madhya Pradesh.

5. Couple, Karle, Maharashtra.

6. Painting : Cave 1, Buddha Visiting Wife and Son, Ajanta Caves, Maharashtra.

7. Devi, Bronze Sculpture, Chola, Tamil Nadu.

8. Mohini, Chennakeshava Temple, Belur, Karnataka.

9. Musicians, Parasurameswara Temple, Bhubaneshwar, Orissa.

10. Painting : Krishna and Radha, Kishangarh.

11. Veena Player, Mukteswara Temple, Bhubaneshwar, Orissa.

12. Nayika, Lingaraja Temple, Bhubaneshwar, Orissa.

13. View Player, Surya Mandir, Konark, Orissa.

Bibliography

Ancient Literature

(a) Sanskrit (Vedic and Classical)

Apastamha Dharmasutra (*Dharmadhikaran*).
Ashwalayana Grihyasutra.
Atharvaveda.
Atri Smriti.
Baudhayana Dharmashastra.
Brihadaranyaka Upanishad.
Brihaspati Smriti.
Brihatsamhita: Varahamihira.
Chhandogya Upanishad.
Devi Bhagavata.
Durga Saptashati.
Garbhopanishad.
Gautama Dharmasutra.
Harita Smriti.
Harsha Charita: Bana.
Ishavasya Upanishad.
Kamasutra: Vatsyayana.
Kautilya Arthashastra.
Kashakritsni (*Kashakritsna*).
Katha Upanishad.
Kaumudi Mahotsava.

Kaushitaki Brahmanopanishad.

Kumara Sambhava: Kalidasa.

Mahabharata: Veda Vyasa.

Mahabhashya: Patanjali.

Maitrayani Samhita.

Malavikagnimitra: Kalidasa.

Manusmriti.

Markandeya Purana.

Mitakshara: Vijnaneshwara.

Mundakopanishad.

Padma Purana.

Paippalada Samhita.

Panchatantra.

Panchika.

Panini Shiksha.

Paniniya Ashtadhyayi.

Purusha Sukta (Rigveda).

Purva Mimansa: Jaimini.

Raghuvamsha: Kalidasa.

Rigveda.

Sahitya Darpana.

Shakuntalam: Kalidasa.

Shatapatha Brahmana.

Shrimad Bhagavata.

Shukla Yajurveda (Rudrashtadhyayi).

Sushruta.

Tattariya Brahmana.

Tattariya Upanishad.

Uttara Ramacharita: Bhavabhuti.

Vaisheshika Sutra: Kanada.

Vajasaneya Brahmana.

Valmikiya Ramayana.

Vishnu Dharmottara Purana.

Vishnu Purana.

Yajnavalkya smriti.

Yajurveda.

Yantra Sarvaswa.

(b) Pali, Prakrita and Apabhransha

Chulla Vagga, Pajapati Pavajja Sutta (*Vinaya Pitaka*).

Etadagga Vagga (*Vinaya Pitaka*).

Hemachandra, Jainacharya.

Siddha Hemachandra (*Shabdanushasana*).

Theri Gatha.

Mediaeval Literature

Prema Tarangini (Sant Suvachana Dasi).

Rama Charita Manasa: Goswami Tulasidasa.

Sahajobai ki Vani (Sant Sahajobai).

Surasagara: Suradasa.

Tiruppavayi (Dravid Sant Andala).

Videha Moksha Prakasha (Sant Suvachana Dasi).

Vijanasagaya (Sant Suvachana Dasi).

Modern Literature

(a) Hindi

Aryon ka Adi Desha: Sampurnananda.

Atmakatha: Mahatma Gandhi, translated by Haribhau Upadhyaya.

Babu ke Quadamon Mein: Rajendra Prasad.

Bharata ka Prachina Itihasa: N.N. Ghosh, translated by C.C. Mani, Indian Press, Allahabad.

Buddha Charya: Rahul Sankrityayana.

Dharmaraja Yudhishthira: Chandra Bali Tripathi: Published by Durgavati Tripathi, Printed at Govind Mudranalaya, Bulanala, Varanasi.

Gita Rahasya athava Karmayoga Shastra: Bal Gangadhar Tilak, translated by Madhav Rao Sapre.

Hind Swarajya: Mahatma Gandhi.

Hindi Sahitya ka Itihasa: Ram Chandra Shukla.

Hindi Vishwakosha: Nagari Pracharini Sabha Varanasi.

Hindu Rajya Shastra: Ambika Prasad Vajpayee.

Hindu Sabhyata: Radhakumud Mukerji (translation).

Hindutva: Ram Das Gaur.

Kinnara Desha Mein: Rahul Sankrityayana.

Mahabharata Mimansa: C.V. Vaidya, Translated by Madhav Rao Sapre, Printed by Indian Press, Allahabad.

Panini Kalina Bharata: Vasudev Sharan Agarwal.

Prachina Bharata ka Itihasa: Rama Shankar Tripathi.

Sarthavaha: Moti Chandra.

Uttara Bharata ki Sant Parampara: Parashuram Chaturvedi.

Vaidic Sahitya: Ram Govind Trivedi, Published by Jnanapitha, Varanasi.

Vedon mein Charkha: D.S. Satvalekar.

Vidhawa Vivaha Khandana: Bhimsen Sharma.

(b) Latin

Naturalis Historia: Pliny, Ed. by C. Meihoff, Leipzig, 1892-1909.

(c) English

Annals and Antiquities of Rajasthan: James Todd.

Cambridge History of India, Pt. I.

Catalogue of the coins of Ancient India (In the British Museum, London, 1936).

Discovery of India: Jawahar Lal Nehru.

Education in Ancient India: A.S. Altekar.

Encyclopedia of Religions and Ethics: Ed. by James Hastings, Edinburgh, 1908.

Epic India: C.V. Vaidya, Mumbai, 1907.

Essays in National Idealism: Anand K. Coomaraswamy.

History of Hindu Dharma Shastra: P.V. Kane.

History of Indian and Indonesian Art: Anand K. Coomaraswamy.

History of Sanskrit Literature: F. Max Mueller.

Importance of Living: Lin Yu Teng.

Indian Art: Vasudev Sharan Agarwal.

Indian Women through the Ages: P. Thomas, Published by P.S. Jayasinghe, Asia Publishing House, Mumbai-1964.

Intercourse between India and the Western World: Rawlinson, H.G., Cambridge, 1916.

Marriage – Past and Present: Mrs. Cole.

Myths and Symbols in Indian Art and Civilization: Heinrich Zimmer.

Position of Women in Hindu Civilization: A.S. Altekar.

Studies in Indian Art: V.S. Agarwal.

The Beginnings of Buddhist Art and Other Essays: A. Fuschs, Translated by L.A. Thomas and F.W. Thomas, Paris and London, 1917.

The Buddhist Cave Temples and their Inscriptions: J. Burgess, Report of the Arch-Survey of Western India, London 1883.

The Cultural Heritage of India: Ramkrishna Centenary Memorial.

The Early History of India: Vincent A. Smith.

The Foundation of Indian Culture: Yogi Aravind.

The Gupta Empire: Radha Kumud Mukerji.

The Hindu View of Art: Mulk Raj Anand.

The Outline of Indian Art: Sir William Orpen.

The Philosophy of Ancient Asiatic Art: Anand K. Coomaraswamy

The Positive Background of Hindu Sociology: Vinay Kumar Sirkar, Allahabad, 1914.

The Women in Rigveda: V.S. Upadhyaya.

(d) German

Deussen, P.: *Philosophie der Upanishads*, Leipzig, 1899.

Fick, R.: *Konigliche Gewalt nach den Dharmasutren*, Leipzig, 1895.

____: *Social Gliederung im nordostliehen Indiaen Zu Buddha's Ziet*, Kiel, 1897.

Winternitz, M.: *Geschichte der Indischen litteratar.*

Index

P

Q

R

T